W9-CBP-766

January 2,000

Happy 50th Birthday David

Love and best wishes from

Norman, Anne-Marie,
Jonathan and Elizabeth.

IMAGES OF
Greater
Manchester

Manchester Evening News

IMAGES OF

Greater

Manchester

The Breedon Books
Publishing Company
Derby

Publisher

First published in Great Britain by The Breedon Books Publishing Company
Limited, 44 Friar Gate, Derby DEl 1DA, 1996

Copyright

Manchester Evening News 1996

All Rights Reserved. No part of this publication may be reproduced, stored in a
retrieval system, or transmitted in any form, or by any means, electronic,
mechanical, photocopying, recording or otherwise without the prior permission
in writing of the Copyright holders, nor be otherwise circulated in any form or
binding or cover other than in which it is published and without a similar
including this condition being imposed on the subsequent publisher.

Compiled by Pam Garside with Tom Waghorn and Lesley Breen.

Acknowledgements

Thanks are due to the original production team of 'Greater Manchester - 125
Years Images from the Manchester Evening News;
Stan Roe, Raymond Coupes, Peter Matthews, Terry Hefferan and Paul Bayley
for format, text and print advice. Ted Stanfield, Richard Howarth and the
Colour Process Department for all photographic reproduction.
To the Systems, Composing and Process department without whom the first
book would never have 'gone to press'.
To all the contributors and supporters.
To the *MEN* Library and Dark Room and all *MEN* photographers past and
present.

Additional material and copy has been provided by Tom Waghorn, Judy
McGiel and the *MEN* Library together with enormous help from the Dark
Room staff and *MEN* Photographers.

ISBN 1 85983 071 4

Printed and bound by Butler & Tanner, Frome, Somerset.
Cover printed by Lawrence Allen, Weston-super-Mare, Avon.
Front cover colour separations by Colour Services, Leicester.

Contents

Foreword

Michael Unger — Editor *Manchester Evening News*

Editorial excellence is my constant goal as editor of the *Manchester Evening News*.

To keep up this standard, to meet all our deadlines and to give our readers what they want is very demanding, but I have an excellent team of journalists, photographers and back-up staff, all of whom take great satisfaction in producing a quality newspaper — 6 days a week!

From campaigns to save our schools, to protecting our children, and to making the environment a better place to live and work — we keep our readers informed and up-to-date with issues that affect us all.

Manchester is the centre of a wonderful region with a great deal to be proud of — and the *Manchester Evening News,* an integral part of its development and success, will be there to report progress.

Edition time at the old Cross Street offices of the *Manchester Evening News* and the fleet of Welsh ponies, harnessed to rubber-tyred high-wheeled carts, wait to carry bundles of the *Evening News* to railway stations and waiting delivery men. These ponies, none more than 15 hands high, were the special joy of early proprietor Mr Russell Allen and were cared for like racehorses at the model stables in Broughton Lane, Salford. Their numbers gradually dwindled owing to the advent of motor-vans, but they were a major form of transporting the newspapers up to March 1952.

Introduction

THIS 1930s picture, by *Manchester Guardian* and *Evening News* photographer Tom Stuttard, illustrates our curiosity to know what is going on, especially in our own corner of the world.

Newspapers prosper despite the advent of radio and television, and this book of pictures with stories and memories celebrates nearly 130 years of a regional newspaper, the *Manchester Evening News,* and the community it serves. It has grown as Greater Manchester has grown and we reflect with pride on some of the region's successes and many strengths. We take you behind the scenes as we look at some of the major news stories and scoops of recent years and give you a brief glimpse of the newspaper operation.

Photographs were chosen from the *News* archives to record places, events, and achievements, but some, such as this one, were included because we just liked them ...and a picture can indeed say a thousand words.

We hope you enjoy this nostalgic journey.

The Manchester Evening News.

No. 1. SATURDAY, OCTOBER 10, 1868. ONE HALFPENNY.

TO THE ELECTORS OF THE CITY OF MANCHESTER.—Gentlemen,—I again respectfully present myself to you as a Candidate for the Representation of my native city in Parliament.

That in so short a time as three weeks nearly 11,000 Electors should have signed a Requisition, pledging themselves to do all in their power to secure my return, is a circumstance unprecedented in the history of our elections, and affords a striking proof of the reality of political convictions in Manchester.

Without attaching a personal significance to this manifestation of your opinion, an explanation is easy:—The contest of last winter has impressed you with the belief that in me you have a sound and honest Liberal, not afraid to express his own political views, whilst he respects the rights and feelings of others; and you probably also think that my commercial connection with the prosperity of this city affords a guarantee for my attention to your local wants and interests.

If I mistake not, the country is determined that the State Church in Ireland—the last badge of conquest and ascendancy—shall cease to exist in that country as an Establishment, and assume the position she has so long occupied in Scotland, and now occupies in the Colonies. If we had forced our religious convictions upon the inhabitants of India, or if the inhabitants of Scotland had not freed themselves from the Episcopal Church so alien to their religious instincts, both India and Scotland would at this moment have been as discontented with English rule as Ireland herself.

I am an attached member of the Church of England, and in favour of the union of Church and State in this country—where that union is real, and based upon the willing assent of the nation; but in my humble opinion to talk of the English and Irish Church standing and falling together, is to echo a false cry, highly dangerous to both.

Mr. Gladstone proposes to secure to Ireland the fabric of her cathedrals and churches, her glebe houses, and all private endowments, as well as carefully to respect all existing rights, and to deal only with the future. In the interests of peaceful government I earnestly hope that these terms will be accepted, and that we shall hear no more of levelling up, nor of universal religious endowment.

Education, both in its higher departments in our universities and in its primary forms in our elementary schools, must become truly national and efficient, with equal rights and privileges for all; but I am not prepared to sanction a system of compulsory education, enforced by the policeman or inspector, until it has been shown that the institution of local boards and local machinery have failed in their objects. Place education within reach of the masses, which has never yet been done, and the boon will be accepted for its own sake.

A real and business-like economy has to be enforced upon the Government, not only by a direct reduction of taxation, but also by a thorough departmental reform, especially in our huge military and naval establishments, so that every pound of expenditure shall represent twenty shillings of efficiency.

The vexatious, and in its practical effect, the cruel restrictions on the exercise of the franchise embodied in the rate-paying clauses of the Reform Bill, must be expunged from the Statute book. A vote once granted should be free, and not attended by penalties based on a sham principle. The idea of a *personal* payment of rates was dropped as untenable, and its operation survives only in a shape which, together with an abolition of rate compounding, is productive of the greatest inconvenience and heart-burning amongst the labouring classes.

I am not opposed to Working Men's Associations. Capital expressed by labour, and capital in money have co-equal rights, and their interests are mutual. Preferential protection of either would be unjust. But I have never been able to understand why the funds of Trades' Unions established and employed for legal purposes should be placed beyond the pale of the law, and be subjected to the depredations of dishonest officials. No question of our time more imperatively demands that both sides should be heard than that connected with the labour market and the capital which is to employ that labour; and if I have the honour to become one of the Representatives of this great industrial community, my earnest endeavours will be given towards the solution of these problems.

I have never liked the principle of secret voting, especially when the restricted franchise heretofore in operation made every voter, as it were, the trustee and representative of many of his neighbours. Now that a vote is placed within the reach of the great body of the people, this objection has become correspondingly weakened, and the mechanical conveniences of the ballot, which are indisputable, may with propriety be considered in future legislation. The true remedy for intimidation, however, is to be found in the comparative equalisation of constituencies, and it seems to me a great reflection on our legislation, and on public opinion itself, if we cannot protect a man in the exercise of his vote whilst he records it in the light of day.

Sanitary reform, and the prevention of avoidable sources of mortality—fortunately for the happiness of mankind—greatly occupy public attention, and have naturally engaged much of my time in the earlier part of my life, and I hope the knowledge thus gained may be useful.

Such, gentlemen, are my political principles, which, being honestly entertained, will be honestly advocated. It is impossible, and if possible, it would be undesirable, that all minor differences should be merged in a stagnant uniformity of opinion. Out of discussion and conflict come truth and advancement, and I am sure the Electors of Manchester will pardon the length at which I have endeavoured to lay before them the grounds of my political faith, desiring as I do, above all things, that there shall be no concealment as to my views.—I am, gentlemen, your faithful and obedient servant,

MITCHELL HENRY.

Portland-street, August 11th, 1868.

REPRESENTATION OF MANCHESTER. CANDIDATURE OF MR. MITCHELL HENRY. ELECTION, 1868.—The Committee for conducting the Election of Mr. Mitchell Henry do hereby give notice to all whom it may concern that they will not be responsible for any expenditure incurred without their consent, nor unless an order signed by the secretary or the election agent of Mr. Henry can be produced as a voucher. That they will not pay for the printing of any placards, circulars, or other documents, nor for the insertion of any advertisements which have not been issued by their authority and do not bear official signatures.

The Committee call the special attention of all electors, ward committees, canvassers, and others interested in the election, to the following provisions of the "Corrupt Practices Prevention Act, 1854":—

"17 and 18 Victoria, cap. 102, sec. 4.—Every candidate at an election who shall corruptly by himself or by or with any person, or by any other ways or means on his behalf, at any time either before, during, or after any election, directly or indirectly, give or provide or cause to be given or provided, or shall be accessory to the giving or providing, or shall pay wholly or in part any expenses incurred for any meat, drink, entertainment, or provision to or for any person in order to be elected or for being elected, or for the purpose of corruptly influencing such person or any other person to give or refrain from giving his vote at such election, or on account of such person having voted or refrained from voting or being about to vote or refrain from voting at such election, shall be deemed guilty of the offence of treating, and shall forfeit the sum of £50 to any person who shall sue for the same, with full costs of suit, and every voter who shall corruptly take or accept any such meat, drink, entertainment, or provision, shall be incapable of voting at such election, and his vote, if given, shall be utterly void and of none effect."

And we hereby give notice to all whom it may concern, that the Committee will not be responsible for any payment or other matters forbidden by the above enactments, or any of them, or anywise made or done in contravention of the same.

H. B. JACKSON, Chairman.
CHAS. DURHAM, } Deputy-Chairmen.
C. P. HENDERSON. }
T. C. DAVIES COLLEY, Election Agent.
JAS. NIELD, Hon. Sec.
Central Committee Rooms, 82, Market-street,
2nd October, 1868.

REPRESENTATION OF MANCHESTER. Mr. MITCHELL HENRY'S COMMITTEE SIT DAILY at 82, Market street. Gentlemen desirous of joining the Committee are respectfully requested to forward their names to the Honorary Secretary.

H. B. JACKSON, Chairman.
CHARLES DURHAM, } Vice-Chairmen.
C. P. HENDERSON, }
J. NIELD, Honorary Secretary.

PROFESSOR FAWCETT, M.P., ON CAPITAL AND LABOUR.

On the subject of trade disputes he said:—"Perhaps of the countless topics comprised by the wide subject upon which I am addressing you, it will be well if I ask you to consider whether any new economic arrangements could be adopted which would cause the wealth of this country to give more general happiness and comfort to the whole nation. The most remarkable characteristic of the mode in which industry is carried on amongst us, is the circumstance that capital is supplied by one class, and that labour is supplied by another class; although capital and labour must combine to produce wealth, yet between those who supply the capital and those who supply the labour there often exists no other relations than those between the buyer and the seller of a commodity. The capitalist, or the employer, on the one hand, and the labourer on the other, struggle keenly to obtain as large a share as possible of the aggregate wealth which results from their combined efforts. This struggle often creates unfriendliness, sometimes strife, and occasionally no settlement can be arrived at, no terms are accepted, war is declared, and every one who has had any experience of a strike knows with what fierceness and determination and at what cost this war is often carried on. We are sometimes prone to forget that there is no reason in the nature of things why there should be this economic separation of classes. In England the land is owned by one class, and the capital which is necessary for its cultivation is owned by another class, and the requisite labour is supplied by a body of men whose poverty I may here parenthetically say is proverbial. This mode of carrying on agriculture does not generally prevail in other countries, but may be considered as almost peculiar to England. The inventions of Arkwright and others caused the destruction of hand-loom weaving. It was found that manufactures could be more profitably carried on on a large scale. Extensive buildings, fitted with costly machinery, represent the investment of a large amount of capital. Hence has arisen our modern industrial system, the leading characteristic of which is a complete separation between capital and labour. From this separation manifold evils arise; where it is essential that there should be unity of effort there is often an antagonism of interest. The employer strives to buy labour as cheaply as possible, the employed endeavour to sell their labour at the highest price; hence we have what is aptly described as a labour market, and in this market there often happens that which daily occurs in every mart where commodities are bought and sold. A merchant who has corn to sell cannot obtain for it such a price as he thinks is fair. He resorts to what may be virtually termed a strike; he warehouses his corn, and withdraws it from the market. Labourers who think they cannot obtain a fair price for their labour, withdraw it from the market, and thus resort to a strike. Many who witness the injury which strikes cause think that the Legislature ought to interfere to prevent them. But it would be as useless and as absurd for the House of Commons to try to forbid labourers withdrawing themselves from the labour market, as it would be to prohibit a merchant warehousing his goods, when he cannot obtain for them a price which he deems reasonable." The tenor of those remarks was to show that strikes could not be prevented by Act of Parliament, but that the cause of the strike being a separation of capital and labour, a remedy for them would be for the labourers to be owners of the capital, the interests of capital and labour would be merged and cease to be antagonistic. "Much of that antagonism of interest, which is the fruitful source of strikes, would be avoided if operatives were allowed directly to participate in profits. This participation may be arranged in various ways. Thus, the Messrs. Crossley, of Halifax, transferred their business into a limited company, the capital of which was £1,650,000; shares representing one-fifth of this capital were reserved for their employées. Workmen were thus enabled to participate in profits, and a certain union between capital and labour was created. The plan has proved eminently successful. The Messrs. Briggs, who are colliery proprietors at Methley, near Leeds, have adopted a plan which effects a more complete union between capital and labour." He believed that courts of arbitration would be only a partial remedy for the evil, though they might be productive of much good. "All will be eager for a change when the evils and the perils resulting from the present state of things are adequately recognised. England has now to carry on in some of her most important branches of industry a keen and closely-contested competition with foreign countries. The slightest additional burden cast upon her may cause the balance to turn against her. Let us, therefore, inquire, 'What are the sources from which peril may come?' At the outset of such an investigation I would lay most emphatic stress upon two maxims. Employers should remember that any deterioration in the condition of our labourers may induce the best and most skilled workmen to emigrate, and the employed should remember that any rise in wages obtained by an undue reduction of their employers' profits may ultimately bring serious loss upon themselves. Capital is always withdrawn from an industry when profits are reduced below the ordinary rate, and capital is the fund from which wages are supplied. It, therefore, becomes evident that on the one hand grave disasters may ensue if employers try to enrich themselves by reducing the earnings of their workmen, or on the other hand, if workmen augment their earnings by diminishing the profits of their employers below the ordinary rate. We, therefore, arrive at the eminently satisfactory conclusion, that those agencies will produce the most permanently beneficial influence, which give additional prosperity to capitalists and labourers alike. I have already shown that such an agency will be brought into operation by the establishment of some system of industrial partnerships."

CONVERTING IRON CUTTINGS INTO BLOOMS.—One always hails with pleasure the utilisation of any waste as so much gained; cotton waste, paper fragments, the washings from woollen factories, have been redeemed from the sewer and the rubbish heap to repay the energy of the inventor, and to supply rising wants with cheap and useful materials: railway grease is in great part supplied by products of the working out of the last of these inventions, and now a very simple and efficacious method of utilising the abundant refuse of the machine shop has just been patented by Mr. Edwd. Hammond Bentall. Iron cuttings, borings, or turnings, are placed in cases of sheet-iron, capable of containing about 1 cwt. of the waste iron; the case, when filled, is submitted to the heat of a reverberatory furnace. When brought to a white heat, it is stamped with stampers, or put under severe pressure, which, owing to the highly-heated and partially-softened state of the metal, will convert it into a solid plastic mass or bloom, possessing a fair grain, and which is capable of being employed for a variety of purposes.

RELICS OF SIR JOHN FRANKLIN'S EXPEDITION.

The *New York Herald* gives the following details of the result, as far as known, of Captain Hall's expedition in search of Sir John Franklin:—

Dr. Goold arrived at New London, Connecticut, a few days since, on board a whaling ship, from Cumberland Inlet, and states that in August, 1867, he spent some considerable time with Mr. Hall, who was then at Repulse Bay. Mr. Hall has traced the fate directly of two of the last survivors of Sir John Franklin's party, and has obtained valuable information regarding the relics and some records reported by the natives to have been left by the lost expedition in King William's Land. Captain Hall learned from some of the Esquimaux, in 1866, that about two years prior to that time Captain Crozier and one of the Franklin crew had died in the vicinity of Southampton Island, while endeavouring to make their way to that place, in the belief that they would be there able to meet a whaler to convey them back to England, or, in fact, anywhere to escape from their arctic prison. Captain Hall is confident of the identity of Captain Crozier with one of the men so described to have perished, as the natives not only gave Captain Crozier's name, but were in possession of certain articles that belonged to him and to his companion. Mr. Hall obtained from these Esquimaux Captain Crozier's watch, a gold chronometer, made by Arnold and Dent, London, besides some small articles of silver and trinkets belonging to their outfit. These relics Mr. Hall now holds, and have been seen and handled by Dr. Goold. Crozier's companion who died with him, is believed to have been a steward of either the Erebus or Terror, as the natives say he was a server of food, but could not recollect his name. The natives also state that they have among them, near Southampton Island, a piece of gold lace and a piece of gold bullion which belonged to Captain Crozier, and is believed to have formed part of one of his epaulettes. They also stated that a number of others had started with Captain Crozier from a place very far north to reach Southampton Inlet, but had perished one by one on the way. They had been passed from one band of Enewits to the other, and when Captain Crozier had passed through two tribes the natives say all further traces were lost, but Captain Hall himself traced the remainder there. Captain Hall also says: "The opinion most entertained is that the natives killed them. They say themselves there was no difficulty in Captain Crozier getting through, because he was accounted among the natives as a first-rate hunter for that country, and could at all times keep himself in food." The records which Captain Hall hopes to be able to secure are in King William's hand, and considerable difficulty is anticipated in the effort to reach them. According to native information the last six survivors built a cairn or rude vault of stones on the rocks, and deposited within it some documents and such articles as they had no further use for, or would have been an encumbrance on their journey. For some time past King William and his tribe have been hostile towards the native followers of King Albert, who inhabit the region about Repulse Bay, where Mr. Hall was quartered, and would allow no incursions into their country. The place where this cairn is described to be situated is about 450 miles northward from Repulse Bay, and in order to reach it Captain Hall has formed an alliance with Albert and his people, and together with his own escort of Europeans, was preparing an expedition of about 90 persons to march in quest of the records. It was Mr. Hall's intention to start in February or March of this year, and he had already accumulated supplies of provisions and other necessaries for the purpose. His force will consist of five Caucasians besides himself, and the remainder would be composed of Alfred's men. Of the whites accompanying him, two were Irish, one German, one Englishman, and one Swede, all of whom were recruited by him from the crew of the Pioneer, which was wrecked in the summer of 1867, at King's Cape. These men are all armed with revolvers and shot guns, and it was mainly through reliance on the Europeans and their weapons that the Albert men were induced to participate in the incursion. Alone they would be unable to cope with King William's forces, who number about two hundred, and could be assembled in a month. Captain Hall would offer no molestation to King William's people, but, if opposed, would give them battle if necessary, as he was determined to obtain the records of the lost explorers if possible. He would be accompanied also by "Joe" and "Hannah," the two Esquimaux or Enewits who, it will be remembered, were a few years ago educated in this country and exhibited in this city. "Joe" and "Hannah" are man and wife, and now form part of Captain Hall's retinue, or household, affording him valuable assistance through their knowledge of the English language in communicating with the various tribes of natives, with whose dialects and peculiarities they are familiar. The entire distance, it was expected, would have to be traversed on sledges drawn by dogs, of which useful motive power Mr. Hall has an abundant stock. It was Mr. Hall's determination, if successful in finding the cairn, and no unforeseen circumstances or obstacles intervened, to press still further forward and if possible reach the open Polar Sea and perhaps return by way of Behring Strait. If impeded he expected to return from his expedition to King William's Land about September of 1868, and take up his quarters for the winter at Repulse Bay. Last year he wintered in this locality, and at the time Dr. Goold saw him was in 66 degrees 28 minutes north latitude, and longitude 81 degrees 5 minutes west.

THE MAN IN THE MOON.—The "man in the moon" has been a nickname for mysterious electioneering agents ever since electioneering was an art. But it had dropped out of use latterly, and was only revived again at the time we speak of. The commissioners who sat in the autumn of 1859 succeeded in pinning this denizen of another planet, and compelling him to appear in human flesh and form. On this occasion he turned out to be a Mr. Whitehead, a tradesman of Bradford; and whether he had or had not been recognised while plying his vocation at Wakefield, it seems really quite impossible to say. He was described by one witness as "a very accomplished man"—a man who never kept his hat on in your company. He was a light-haired, pleasant-looking man, sometimes with a beard, sometimes not; but nobody knew who he was. Scores of electors were bribed by him in the openest manner, and hundreds tempted. In fact, Wakefield appears to have been nearly as bad as Saint Albans. In this instance the bribery was of the most wholesale and unguarded character. The evidence is very amusing. Money there was called sugar; and the reception of it, having your hand scratched. The rival candidates were Leatham, Liberal, and Charlesworth, Conservative. One John Jackson had his hand scratched with thirty pounds' worth of the luscious article; but, as thirty-five had been promised, the only effect was to lose his vote and convert him into an active enemy at the same time. His wife, indeed, propitiated by the artful compliment of a Leathamite, to the effect that "women could do anything," tried to persuade her husband to vote for the Liberals; but the more practical Jackson, finding his sugar short weight, soothed his conscience and gratified his vengeance at the same time by voting for Charlesworth. These miscarriages of injustice were not infrequent. We read of "Peter the Jew," who was employed to bribe George Senior, and who, with the cupidity of his race, stopping two pounds out of the money, lost his party the vote in consequence. We find, likewise, that even the great men of all, he of the moon, was occasionally baffled by the dishonesty or astuteness of his customers. "A lady" sold a ham to him for twenty-five pounds, engaging that her husband, who was a Liberal, should vote Conservative; but this heroic woman, more jealous for her husband's honour than her own, kept both the secret and the money, whereby her husband voted with his conscience, and she had "twelve new dresses."—*Cassell's Magazine.*

BEAUTY AND BRAINS.

That lovely woman fulfils only half her mission when she is unpersonable instead of beautiful, all young men, and all pretty girls secure in the consciousness of their own perfections, will agree. Indeed, it is cruel to hear the way in which heady youth despises ugly girls or fading women, however clever, whose charm lies in their cleverness only, with a counteraction in their plainness. To hear them, one would think that hardness of feature, like poverty, was a crime voluntarily perpetrated, and that contempt was a righteous retribution for the offence. Yet their preference, though so cruelly expressed, is to a certain extent the right thing. When we are young, the beauty of women has a supreme attraction beyond all other possessions or qualities, and there are self-evident reasons why it should be so.

It is only as we grow older that we know the value of brains, and, while still admiring beauty—as, indeed, who does not—admire it as one passing by on the other side; as a grace to look at, but not to hold, unless accompanied by something more lasting. This is in the middle term of a man's life. Old age, perhaps with the unconscious yearning of regret, goes back to the love of youth and beauty for their own sake; extremes meeting here as in almost all other circumstances. The danger is when a young man, obeying the natural impulse of his age and state, marries beauty only, with nothing of more durable wear beneath. The mind sees what it brings, and we love the ideal we create rather than the reality that exists. A pretty face, the unworn nerves of youth, the freshness of hope that has not yet been soured by disappointment or chilled by experience, a neat stroke at croquet, and a merry laugh easily excited, made a girl a goddess to a boy who is what he himself calls in love and his friends call spoony. She may be narrow, selfish, spoiled, unfit to bear the burdens of life, and unable to meet her trials patiently; she may be utterly unpractical and silly.

Many a man has cursed, his whole life long, the youthful infatuation that made him marry. Take the case of a rising politician, whose fair-faced wife is either too stupid to care about his position, or else who imperils it by her folly. If amiable and affectionate, and in her own silly little way ambitious, she does him incalculable mischief by exaggeration, and by saying and doing exactly the things that are most damaging to him; if stupid, she is just so much dead weight that he has to carry with him while swimming up the stream. She is very lovely, certainly, and people crowd her drawing-room to look at her; but a plain-featured, sensible, shrewd woman, with no beauty to speak of, but with tact and cleverness, would have helped him in his career far better than would Venus herself if brainless. And so he finds out, when it is too late, to change M for N in the marriage service.

Men do not care for brains in excess in women. They like a sympathetic intellect which can follow them, and seize their thoughts as quickly as they are uttered, but they do not much care for any clear or special knowledge of facts; and even the most philosophic among them would rather not be set right in a classical quotation, an astronomical calculation, or the exact bearing of a political question by a lovely being in tarlatane whom he was graciously unbending to instruct. Neither do they want anything very strong-minded. To most men, indeed, the feminine strongmindedness that can discuss immoral problems without blushing, and despise religious observances as useful only to weak souls, is a quality as unwomanly as a well-developed biceps or a huge fist would be. It is sympathy, not antagonism; it is companionship, not rivalry, still less supremacy, that they like in women; and some women with brains as well as learning—for the two are not the same thing—understand this, and keep their blue stockings well covered by their petticoats. Others, enthusiasts for the freedom of thought and intellectual rights, show theirs defiantly, and meet with their reward. Men shrink from them. Even clever men, able to meet them on their own ground, do not feel drawn to them, while all but high-class minds are dwarfed and humiliated by their learning and their moral courage. And this is what no man likes to feel in the presence of a woman, and because of her superiority. But the brains most useful to women, and most befitting their work in life, are those which show themselves in common sense, in good judgment, and that kind of patient courage which enables them to bear small crosses and great trials alike with dignity and good temper.

A Madrid correspondent of the *Independance* anticipates an interregnum of five or six months, to be followed by the appointment of a foreign Sovereign. He anticipates that the choice of the nation will devolve on the King of Portugal, possibly on a Belgian Prince, or even on "one of the sons of the Queen of England."

THE MUNICIPAL ELECTION.—There are already signs of a contest in some of the Manchester wards in anticipation of next month's elections, and it is not unlikely that party politics will form a prominent feature in the struggle. It is said that among the retiring councillors there are those who have offended their constituents by attending more to the defence of the Irish Church than to the local interests of the citizens. Be that as it may, two of the retiring representatives who are noted "Constitutionalists," viz., Mr. George Anderton in Collegiate Ward, and Mr. Jonn Townsend in St. Clement's Ward are threatened with serious opposition. The former has an opponent in Mr. Wm. Scott Brown (of the firm of Jewsbury and Brown, chemists, Market-street). Mr. Brown addressed the municipal electors at the Merchants' Hotel, Oldham-street. There was a numerous and respectable assembly, and the chair was occupied by Mr. Josiah Taylor. Mr. Brown, in the course of his speech, said he was in favour of an education scheme based upon local taxation and local management, and unsectarian; he should pay particular attention to the sanitary and health committees, and do all he could to diminish the death rate. In answer to questions, he said he would not vote for the reduction of the Town-clerk's salary by one-half; he would support any motion that might be brought forward for the separation of the poor-rates from the borough-rates.—On the motion of Mr. J. Little, seconded by Mr. T. Peel, a resolution, pledging the meeting to assist in securing Mr. Brown's return, was carried unanimously.

PUNISHMENT FOR ADULTERATION OF FOOD IN LONDON IN THE MIDDLE AGES.—In the "Memorials of London," we find that in 1311, a baker was arrested for selling putrid bread, and in 1316 another baker was sentenced to be drawn on a hurdle through the principal streets of the city for selling "light bread deficient in weight;" and in the same year the punishment of the pillory was inflicted upon a man and a woman for selling bread of "rotten materials," and deficient in weight. In 1319 a certain William Spelyng was adjudged to be put upon the pillory, and two putrid beef carcases to be burnt under him for exposing the said carcases for sale; and in 1320 we find two cases similar to the preceding. In 1348 and 1353 the punishment of the pillory was inflicted for selling carrion,—in one case the meat being burnt under the offender. In 1351, proclamations were issued as to the sale of fish. In 1364, a seller of unsound wine was punised by being made to drink it. In the following year the punishment of the pillory was inflicted upon a poulterer for selling putrid pigeons. In 1372 a woman was punished for selling putrid soles; the fish was ordered to be burnt, and the cause of her punishment proclaimed; and we find another case of punishment by the pillory in 1381 for exposing putrid pigeons for sale. In 1390, twelve barrels of eels were ordered to be taken out of the city, and buried in some place underground, lest the air might become infected through the stench arising therefrom. An important proclamation against the adulteration and mixing of wines was issued by Henry V., in 1419, and the punishment of the pillory was ordered for all who sold false wines. If a few examples similar to the above kind were made at the present day they would be of service to the community.

A reproduction of the first issue of the *Manchester Evening News*.

The birth of the News

IF you were a Liberal candidate in 1868, and experiencing great difficulty in obtaining good reports of your meetings in the existing papers, it might seem a logical move to start your own electioneering news sheet.

And, like many others, the man who was to become the founder of the *Manchester Evening News* did just this. Mitchell Henry was born in Ardwick in 1833, the son of a well-known textile merchant. He was an eminent consulting surgeon, deeply concerned about the state of sanitation and public health in Britain. On the death of his father, he relinquished his medical career to take over the family business and, when all was running smoothly, he turned to politics to try to improve standards.

On October 10, 1868, the first eight-page issue of his electioneering broadsheet was published and given out at a celebration dinner at the Woolsack Hotel. It went on sale for one halfpenny at 3pm each day.

This first issue, and all others up to election day, published Mr Henry's election pledge on the front page and gave reports of his meetings, plus names of his supporters and committee members. The appointed editor, Mr T.Broscombe, made a serious attempt at injecting newsworthy items such as reports of the Liverpool and Manchester Stock Markets, readers' letters and even advertisements before election day on Tuesday, November 17. On this day, according to the paper, Henry made a noble act of self sacrifice and, at 1pm, retired from the contest to prevent a catastrophe to the Liberal cause. Perhaps if he had started the *Manchester Evening News* a few months earlier, he might have stood a better chance of success. As it was, he decided to sell his broad sheet to John Edward Taylor, son of J.E.Taylor who was the first proprietor of the *Manchester Guardian*, and his brother-in-law Peter Allen.

It is interesting to note that Mr Henry became a member of Parliament for County Galway three years later and did important work for Irish agriculture.

The leading article in the first issue of the *Manchester Evening News* began: "In putting ourselves into print we have no apology to offer, but the assurance of an honest aim to serve public interests..."

This aim has continued throughout the twentieth century and the words are still just as valid today.

Here we see a nineteenth-century scene on a busy Manchester street with a young newspaper seller.

The Examiner building in Pall Mall, Manchester, later to be demolished to make room for the new *Manchester Guardian* and *Evening News* building in 1929.

Early days

IN 1868 the world was on the threshold of a new era and the Liberals were being swept to power after promising to set afoot a vast new range of social reforms.

And in Manchester, central powerhouse of the industrial revolution, was being mirrored the first of those reforms as the exaggerated individualism of the early Victorian years gave way to the collective state.

The death rate in Manchester that year was the highest in Britain – a grim tribute to the develop-ment of a typical nineteenth-century industrial city. But Manchester appointed its first Medical Officer of Health, Dr Leigh, who made it his first task to examine the city's unenviable position as one of the most unhealthy towns in the Kingdom.

Something at last was about to be done. And indeed, not all of the city was ailing. Opportunity abounded as the British Empire reached the peak of its power and fortunes were to be made in the north.

The picture which makes the Edwardian era come alive. All the daytime hustle and bustle of the Peter Street section of Manchester's theatreland of the early 1900s. On the right is the Comedy Theatre, farther down on the same side is the Grand. On the other side is the Theatre Royal, then the Free Trade Hall and the Tivoli.

Drinks are a halfpenny or penny a glass at the poultry market, Shudehill, Manchester.

Lunch break outside Sacred Trinity Church on Salford's famous 'Flat Iron' market.

For women the shawl was obligatory – as was their misery.

Right: These two young girls with their white 'pinnies' have just been to the 'jug and bottle' shop for jugs of beer.

Passers-by study the wares at Salford's 'Flat Iron' market.

A Victorian fair among the chimneys and warehouses of Manchester. The photographer has skilfully captured the wistful expression and poverty-stricken air of the children.

A picture from a reader shows a general store in Greengate, Salford.

Decked out in May Day Parade finery is one of Paulden's horse-drawn delivery vans. William Paulden, a showman as well as a shrewd businessman, attracted customers to his Stretford Road shop by spectacular window displays, sometimes with live lions and tigers. A draper, he also sold stout furniture and hard-wearing lino at cheap prices.

Wilsons, a grocer's shop in Regent Road, Salford.

Shire horses pull the carts in this early morning turnout.

Strong men and sturdy horses - it took both to deliver barrels of beer. These drivers and their dray carts are seen outside the brewery of J. W. Lees at Middleton Junction, early in the reign of King George V. For all their rugged, no-nonsense appearance, men like this often had great affection for their horses. On May Day each year, when every horse was specially groomed and decorated, the animals made a splendid sight on the streets of Manchester.

The Cotton Exchange is in the distance and the Grosvenor Hotel on the right-hand side of the picture.

The Manchester Palace in times when the music hall was at its peak and the open-top tramcar was still one of the kings of the road. In the distance is St Peter's Church.

An early drawing of the *Manchester Guardian* and *Evening News* Building in Cross Street. The close links with the *Manchester Guardian* continued and were strengthened in 1924 when John Russell Scott bought the *Manchester Evening News*. The two papers were brought together under one ownership, while maintaining their individuality and editorial independence. The paper was printed at Cross Street until 1970 when the company moved to premises on Deansgate.

St Ann's Square in the 1890s with a line up of hansom cabs.

Trilbies, bowlers and flat caps in Bank Street, Manchester. And the *Evening News* is on sale as usual.

A bustle of activity at the top of a relatively prosperous looking Cross Street where horse-drawn trams and carts dominate the scene in this early photograph.

1884, and a steamer takes on passengers on the River Irwell near Manchester Cathedral. Chetham's School is in the background. Sailings to Pomona Gardens were very popular with courting couples, who liked to watch the eel-catchers, admire views of Trafford Park woodlands and gaze at the peaceful farms and orchards. But the increasing smells from the river stopped it all. Fishing in the Irwell ended about 1850 (an 18lb salmon was caught near Warrington in 1840).

They brought the sea to Manchester's doorstep

COURAGE and enterprise built the Manchester Ship Canal.

Towards the end of the 19th century, Manchester was declining fast as a city. One reason was that the railways were charging nearly twice as much as those on the Continent. But even more damaging were the ever-growing charges and dock dues at Liverpool.

For an Oldham spinner it was cheaper to buy cotton in Germany or France, ship it to Hull, and then send it by rail to Oldham, than to buy in Liverpool.

Manchester had to find an answer or die.

It took three years to push and coax the necessary Bill through Parliament and when at last Daniel Adamson, who had set the scheme rolling, came home successful from London, workers took the horses from his carriage and dragged him home, cannons were fired, church bells rang and bands played.

Raising the money was the next struggle. One necessary item even before the work could start was the purchase of the Bridgewater Navigation Company's property and the £1,710,000 cheque for that was the largest ever drawn up to that time.

Enough finance was arranged to justify going on, and on November 11, 1887, Lord Egerton of Tatton, who succeeded Adamson as chairman of the Manchester Ship Canal Company, cut the first sod at Eastham. Then, with work well under way, the weather brought new worries. Unprecedented storms and floods destroyed overnight the work of months. Again a few months later, more storms left six miles of excavated canal bed 40 feet under water in places. Ice and snow followed.

All this meant extra expense, and to make matters worse, the Bridgewater Canal, the only profit-making asset the directors had, was frozen and out of action. More money was needed, and there was no time to raise it by public appeal. So it came about that Manchester City Council unanimously approved assistance to the extent of £3 million. Then in 1892 it was reported that another £1¼ million was necessary to finish the work. To be on the safe side, the City Council made £2 million available, with the proviso that the Corporation should have a majority on the Board of Directors.

The Manchester Ship Canal celebrated its centenary in 1994 with a year of special events.

Navvies digging Manchester Ship Canal: 16,000 of them were employed on the project known as 'the Big Ditch'.

23

Placing sandstone pitching on the canal bank.

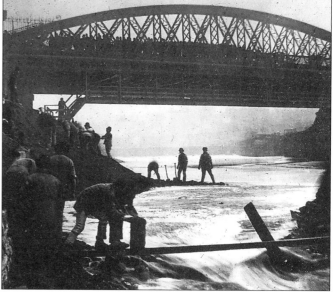

Barton Bridge under construction.

A bucket dredger.

Splitting rock for removal and re-use as pitching on canal banks.

The inside of one of the syphons carrying the River Gowy under the canal at Stanlow, Ellesmere Port.

One of the steel lattice booms of a railway viaduct under construction.

Driving piles to form Coffer dam.

Shropshire Union Canal lighthouse at Ellesmere Port.

Dutch fascine workers labouring on the canal banks.

Steam grab removing excavation.

Original pumping station at Eastham locks.

Inspecting the Weaver sluices.

Manchester received a royal visit after the opening of the Ship Canal. Streets and buildings along the eight-mile route of the procession were gaily decorated. Seen here is a triumphal arch of fire escape ladders over Deansgate. Two million people turned out to cheer the Queen on that day.

The first big ships sailed up to Manchester on January 1, 1894, and on May 21, 1894, the official opening was performed by Queen Victoria on board the yacht *Enchantress*. This painting commemorated the occasion. The total cost of the canal was about £15 million. In the first year 925,000 tons of traffic entered the Port of Manchester, 1896 saw that figure doubled.

The Canal brought in the expected new trade. Warehouses and offices mushroomed around Manchester Docks and Trafford Park. On the left is the entrance to the Park in 1905 when the No.9 dock was opened on the site of the New Barns racecourse.

They fought in the Boer War

1899 The Boer War – The dead and the injured lie in the trenches as the soldiers fight on from behind the barricades.

A blindfolded emissary is brought to discuss terms of surrender after the Boer defeat at Paaderberg.

Victoria, the end of an era

NEWS. DEATH OF THE QUEEN.

RECORD OF A NOBLE LIFE.

SPECIAL MEMOIR.

With profound regret we have to announce that the illness of Her Majesty the Queen has terminated fatally.

The death of Queen Victoria was recorded on page three of the newspaper on January 22, 1901. After a reign of over 50 years, when the majority of Britons had known no other monarch, it was the end of a momentous era. The days of the Empire were already fading with the Boer War and conflict in India and the dark days of World War One were not far ahead.

The Boer War dragged out from 1899 to 1902, and there were many celebrations when it ended like this procession seen in Portland Street. But much livelier jubilation had marked some of the turning-points of the war, and one of them even gave a new word to the language – 'Mafficking'.

Early reporting staff

AS with all great newspapers, the reputation of the *Manchester Evening News* has been built up on a succession of resourceful, far-sighted editors and on succeeding generations of newsmen – reporters, photographers, sub-editors – dedicated to the single-minded task of keeping their newspaper ahead of the news.

After Mr T.Broscombe, Hugh Wilson was appointed editor and was paid £3 per week for his services. The reporter – only one in those early days – received 25 shillings.

James Parkinson, a long-serving editor held the position for many years and was passionately fond of cricket. He saw little purpose in any other sport and preferred his reporters to be similarly enthusiastic.

He was succeeded by W.A.Balmforth, who served the paper with distinction for over 25 years. It was under his direction that the *News* began to take shape as a family newspaper with the aim to keep its columns clean and wholesome, while still reporting important, if sometimes distasteful news.

Balmforth was followed by Henry Archer who, in the late twenties made the revolutionary decision to put news instead of adverts on the front page.

Then came W.J.Haley who re-shaped the paper and it was under his editorship that the *Manchester Evening News* made enormous strides. By 1939 it had become the biggest evening paper outside London and still maintains a huge and loyal readership today.

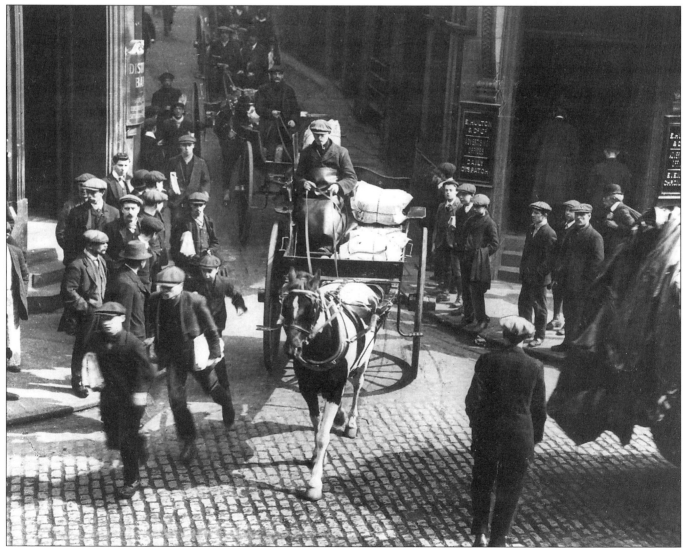

3.00 pm and the 'pony expresses' tear out of Cross Street and into Market Street to the delight of bystanders.

FROM THE
"MANCHESTER EVENING NEWS" REPORTING STAFF. 1903-4.
TO THEIR CHIEF. MR W. A. BALMFORTH. XMAS. 1904.

This unusual group picture, which shows all the members of an early reporting staff of the *Manchester Evening News* in 1903 with their Editor William Balmforth, was presented on March 5, 1904 at the Dorchester Hotel, London where the jubilee dinner of the National Union of Journalists was held. The Union was founded in Manchester in 1906, and the actual founder, W.N.Watts (No.9), became its first general secretary. This picture is unique because, not only are several of the original or early officials of the Union shown, but every member of staff was at some time in one or other of Press causes, the National Union of Journalists, the Institute of Journalists, the Newspaper Press Fund, or the Manchester Press Club.

The professional photographer at work: The large camera on sturdy tripod, and equally sturdy packing case for the operator to stand on. The occasion was the inauguration of Manchester's first electrified tram route on June 6, 1901. The line of new electric trams, bedecked with flowers and potted palms and filled with top-hatted and bewhiskered City Fathers made its way from Albert Square to Cheetham Hill, where the Lord Mayor officially opened the Queen's Road Depot.

A red-letter day at Walkden - the first tramcar arrives, on June 22, 1906. The crowd is 'working class', but note that even the schoolboys are wearing stiff collars.

Trams they all loved

FROM 1865 Manchester had enjoyed a flourishing public transport service run with the unified control of the Manchester Carriage Company. By 1870 there were three-horse omnibuses providing services along most of the city's main roads. But they were still the transport of the well-to-do. After the introduction of carriages drawn by horses in 1877 in both Manchester and Salford, the tramcar became an institution. In 1901 the first motorised tramcar made its appearance and within two years, in a massive undertaking, almost the whole of the system had been converted to electric traction. It became an affordable means of transport for all.

Standing room only! One of the first trams arrives at Albert Square, Manchester, to pick up passengers.

It is 3.30pm on June 12, 1906, as crowds line the street at Sale Moor village to greet 496, the special car which opened the new route.

King Edward VII and Queen Alexandra arrive on July 13, 1905, for the unveiling of the Lancashire Fusiliers monument in Oldfield Road, Salford.

When General Booth founded his Salvation Army in 1878, he and his followers were regarded as a nuisance and trouble makers. By 1902 the value of his work was officially recognised when King Edward VII invited him to be present at his Coronation. In 1910 the General made an almost royal progress through Eccles as this *News* picture of the time shows.

Manchester turns out to greet their Royal Highnesses King George V and Queen Mary on their State visit to the city on July 14, 1913.

The Royal progression route passed Piccadilly where a crowd gathered to watch, many perched dangerously on the roofs and balconies of the buildings to get a better view.

Here are the residents of Silk Street, Salford, posing for the camera at the street party held in honour of the Coronation of King George V on June 22, 1911.

Belle Vue was a popular entertainment centre opened in 1835 by another visionary, Arthur Jennison. It held many attractions, including a zoo, and was set amid beautiful gardens. The picture shows the Chinese tearoom.

An unusually posed group of members of the Manchester Fire Brigade at their headquarters in Jackson's Row in 1898.

These were times of unrest and here we see a detachment of police from Oldham having just arrived at Victoria Station for strike duty in Manchester in August, 1911.

Advertising has played an enormous part in the success of the *Manchester Evening News*. From as early as the sixth issue in 1868, advertisements started to appear. In November of the same year a notice giving a 'classification of advertisements' was published. For 'tuppence' per line – paid prior to insertion, readers could advertise for Situations – Apartments, vacant or wanted – Money to be 'lent' or wanted – Partnerships – Houses – and Sales by Private Contract. These adverts were a great selling point for the paper and appeared on the front page. The leader column and news appeared on page three. Even important news items such as the death of Queen Victoria, as we saw earlier, was consigned to the inner pages.

Votes for women

Mrs Emmeline Pankhurst being removed by the law during a demonstration at Buckingham Palace gates.

Mrs Pankhurst is on the right with Mrs Baines of Stockport who shared imprisonment with her.

Famous suffragette Mrs Emmeline Pankhurst made her entry into political life as the bride of Dr Pankhurst who was one of the founders of the Women's Suffrage Society.

As his wife she gained confidence by helping him in his work and after his death, with her daughters Christabel and Sylvia plus a few women friends formed the Women's Social and Political Union.

She was arrested twelve times and jailed on several occasions. She died at the age of 70 in 1928 after having lived just long enough to see the passing of the Act which gave full and equal suffrage to men and women.

Her house in Plymouth Grove, Manchester, is now a museum.

On the left, standing with Christabel Pankhurst, is Mary Cawthorp a Yorkshire organiser, who started the protest in the House of Commons. On the extreme right in the trap is Adela Pankhurst, daughter of Christabel.

When Henry Ford decided to expand into the English car market with his highly popular and affordable Model T, he chose Manchester as his base, opening his factory and shop in Trafford Park in 1911.

All gleaming and new these Ford cars and vans are lined up outside the factory in Trafford Park. In just one day 100 cars were produced.

Rolls and Royce

Frederick Henry Royce.

The Hon Charles Stewart Rolls.

The world renowned Rolls-Royce. Henry Royce built his first 10hp 2-cylinder Royce motor car at his factory in Cooke Street, Manchester in 1904. A year later he met investor the Hon Charles Stuart Rolls in the Midland Hotel and the Rolls-Royce company was formed. The 40hp Silver Ghost was soon designed and made the firm world famous. His engines also powered early aircraft and are still regarded as the most reliable engines in the world.

Was this a rally of Rolls-Royce cars? Whatever the occasion, it brought four models together at the summit of the Buxton-Macclesfield Road, outside the Cat and Fiddle Inn.

Brothers Alliott Verdon-Roe (left) and Humphrey V Roe in earlier days with their wood and canvas aircraft.

An Avro Type E being transported through Manchester in 1910.

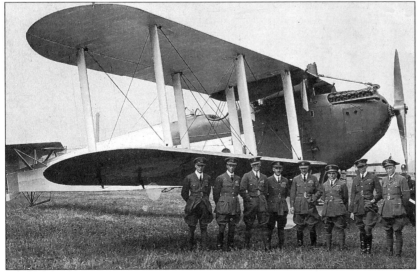

The new Avro Aldershot giant bomber 850 photographed at Alexandra Park where, along with another similar machines after final tests, have been taken over by the RAF. These machines were all metal.

The high flyers of AVRO

Alliott Verdon-Roe, the pioneer flyer and aeroplane builder was born in 1877 in Patricroft.

An engineer and designer, his spare time interest was building model aircraft, which he entered for competitions. He also corresponded with the Wright Brothers in America on the subject of gliding.

One of his brothers, Humphrey was a partner in a surgical webbing company in Brownsfield Mill, Great Ancoats Street and offered finance for a full scale powered aeroplane named The Bullseye after a brand of gents braces manufactured by Horace. On July 13, 1909 with Alliot at the controls, it made a flight of 100ft, which is accepted by many authorities as the first recorded flight by a British flyer in a British built machine.

The first planes were constructed at the Mill by the newly formed AVRO company and advertising at the time stated that 'AVRO planes are held up by Bullseye braces'.

For the war, the factory supplied Gnome engined biplanes to the Central Flying School and in 1913 production was transferred to a site in Clifton Street, Miles Platting, where the famous AVRO 504 biplane became the standard product. It was designed by Roy Chadwick, architect of the World War Two Lancaster Bomber.

An Avro in action in World War One.

Gallant Colonel Cody and his biplane photographed in Blackpool in 1910 by Walter Doughty a celebrated *News* photographer. The plane, a flimsy thing of bamboo and canvas is being swept away by a gust of wind while Cody and his helpers desperately try to hold it. A moment later it overturned completely and was a crumpled wreck. Such were the trials and tribulations of these early aviators.

Your country needs you

A recruiting officer finds a not too willing listener during a recruiting campaign in Manchester during World War One.

IT was a perfect summer that year of 1914, which was only as it should be, for it was to mark the end of an era and set the world on a trail of war and disaster on a scale never imagined.

The first lightning flash came late in June, when an Austrian Archduke was killed by an assassin's bullet. That was the spark that set alight the powder kegs of World War One.

This was to be the war to end all wars, and our armies were to return to a land fit for heroes to live in. Alas, it was no such thing, and the years following the war were years of poverty, of depression, of unemployment and hunger.

Men of the 1st Lancashire Fusiliers fixing bayonets before the assault on Beaumont-Hamel, on July 1, 1916. The battalion had 483 casualties that day with 180 officers and men killed.

On March 21, 1915 – Exactly three years to the day before the Battle of Manchester Hill was fought – the 16th Manchesters marched past Lord Kitchener at Manchester Town Hall with the rest of the City Battalions.

1919 – Coming home: Men of the 8th Battalion The Manchester Regiment marching along London Road, Manchester, on their return from Belgium. Captain Stewart is leading.

Broughton House, Salford was created in 1916 as a home for ex-servicemen and still exists today. The money for the home was raised by Colonel Sir William Coates who also formed a company of stretcher bearers for the Boer War and later helped form the Territorial Army.

Following World War One, Captain John William Alcock, DSC (left), and Lieutenant Arthur Whitton-Brown put their dreams to practical test, and made them come true by making the first non-stop Transatlantic flight, 1,950 miles in 15 hours and 57 minutes from Newfoundland to Ireland.

King George and Queen Mary, with Princess Mary, during their visit on October 8, 1921, to open the reconstructed Royal Exchange. On the left of the Lord Mayor, Alderman W. (later Sir William) Kay is the Recorder, Mr A.H.Ashton, KC. To the right of the Lady Mayoress is the Town Clerk, Mr T.Hudson. Lord Derby is behind Queen Mary, and on the left is Chief Constable, Sir Robert Peacock.

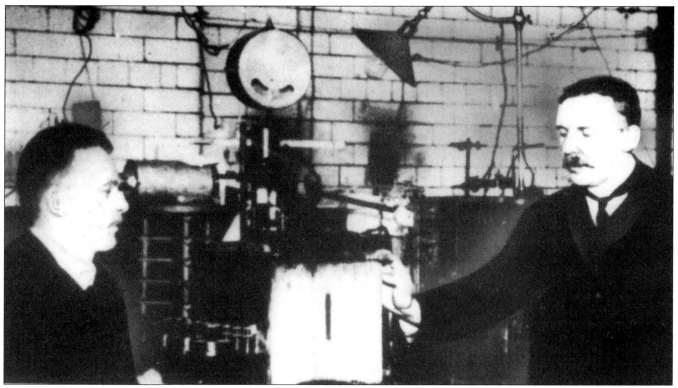

Rutherford and Geiger (left) counting alpha-rays in Manchester. Ernest Rutherford was a professor of physics at Manchester University who, in 1918, headed the team which first split the atom. One of his valuable collaborators at the university was Hans Geiger, the inventor of the first version of the particle counter, who joined the staff from Germany.

Manchester Whit Walks which took place during Wakes Week were the highlight of the year. The children, dressed in their 'Sunday best' paraded through the streets. Our picture shows an Italian Society group, carrying a statue of the Madonna and Child.

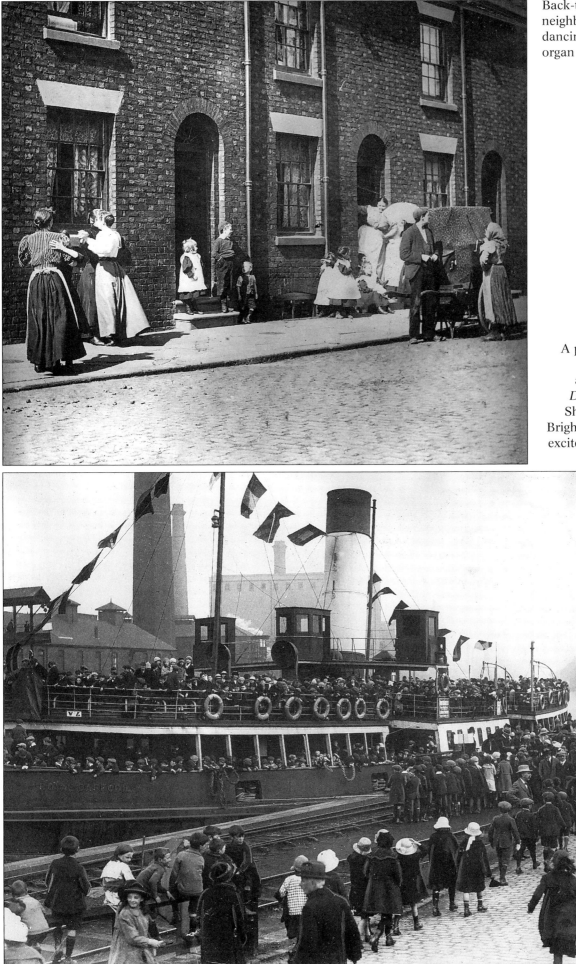

Back-to-back neighbourliness and dancing to a barrel organ in the street.

A popular outing in 1928 was a trip aboard the *Royal Daffodil* along the Ship Canal to New Brighton. Here we see excited children going aboard.

Dressed in their 'Sunday best' visitors to Buile Hill Park in Pendleton enjoyed the music from the Band Stand.

Another popular pastime was cycling, and here we see a club pedalling through Alderley Edge. Note the ladies' smart hats and long skirts.

Heartbreaking though unemployment can be, it was even grimmer in the 1930s when the dole was pitifully small and to be out of work meant that families went hungry. Full scale protest marches were organised in the main cities including Manchester. These pictures show some of the scenes at this sad time.

With miners on strike in 1926, women with scarves round their heads, and a boy search a spoil heap near Manchester for fuel.

An inevitable part of the industrial scene, the strike pickets. These at Burnley in October 1931 look more weary than militant, but the women raise a smile for the press photographers.

This street is typical of the living conditions in the early thirties. It was listed for demolition under a slum clearance scheme.

A view of a traffic jam in Manchester. A patient horse in the foreground is pulling a load of 'Quinine Champagne' and a lorry loaded with cotton waste follows a *Manchester Evening News* van to head up Market Street.

The mounted police had to control the crowds of men waiting hopefully near Aytoun Street 'labour exchange'.

There were many ugly incidents. Here the Manchester Fire Brigade returns from a riot incident in Market Street.

An orderly protest march against unemployment, at the junction of Portland Street and Oxford Street, Manchester.

When 30 jobs were advertised for Queen's Park Hippodrome, Harpurhey, a queue of over 1,000 people had formed before midday.

'Passengers for tramcars and buses must form a queue' said a new regulation made in 1933. The law was not always obeyed as our photographer records in Albert Square the same day.

On the morning of September 26, 1931, Mahatma Gandhi, the Hindu politician and leader of the National Congress party in India, visited Darwen. He was the guest of Charles Haworth of Darwen. Gandhi was assassinated by a Hindu fanatic in 1948.

A 1931 view of the Manchester Central Library beginning to take shape in St Peter's Square. The Waldorf Restaurant and St Peter's Hotel originally stood on this site.

King George V and Queen Mary at the entrance of the City's new Central Library in 1934, as they perform the official opening ceremony.

An advertisement from the paper promotes the film *The Love Parade* starring Maurice Chevalier and Jeanette MacDonald at the Paramount Theatre.

One of the Manchester city centre cinemas which never really made it. The Piccadilly, next to the State Café was a popular teatime rendezvous in the thirties.

Here is C.B.Cochrane with some of his principals arriving for rehearsals of his review *Streamline* which opened at the Opera House. With 'C B' are (left to right) Miss Florence Desmond, Miss Nora Howard and Madamoiselle Meg Leconnier.

Musical impresario, C.B.Cochrane (left) outside the Midland Hotel talking to composer, Cole Porter.

At a gathering at the Paramount Theatre in October 1937, we see (from the left) Herbert Wilcox, Sybil Thorndike, Anna Neagle and Marie Burke.

Singer and film star Gracie Fields with the Mayor of Rochdale during her visit in 1931.

Jessie Matthews and her husband Sonnie Hale meet some of the girls dressed for a tableaux in costumes of all nations before performing the opening ceremony at the gala launching of the Gaumont.

Amy, Wonderful Amy... Britain's queen of the air, Amy Johnson who became Mrs Jim Mollison arriving at Barton Aerodrome on a visit to Manchester on October 31, 1931.

On July 17, 1934, King George V's visit to Manchester was both a military and civic occasion. As Colonel-in-Chief of the Manchester Regiment he was presented with a set of silver drums from Lord Mayor Samuel Woolam. Later the same day the King laid the foundation stone of the Town Hall extension and officially opened the new Central Library.

Manchester University Rowing Club's boat looks far too big a load for this small car which took it from Manchester over the Pennines for York Regatta.

On December 10, 1936 after the shortest reign in British history, Edward VIII shocked the nation by renouncing the Throne for himself and his descendants. He wished to marry divorcee Mrs Wallis Simpson which was not acceptable for a King of England. On 3 June, 1937, one year after his abdication they were married in France at the Chateau de Caude where they were photographed by Cecil Beaton.

These ladies of Walter Street, Harpurhey get ready for the Coronation of George VI, the shy brother of the popular Edward VIII who had abdicated the previous year. The flags are hung across the street, the roads are swept and the pavements are scrubbed clean ready for the festivities

In Manson Street, Ardwick Green this street party is in full swing as the children wave for the camera.

One of Manchester's most distinguished shopping streets is impressively decked out in white and gold banners for the Coronation of King George VI.

Pre-war memories

Bob Corfield – From copy boy in 1934 to proof reader and then staff photographer. He retired in 1984. Here are some of his pre-war memories.

MY first encounter with the *MEN* was way back in 1934 when I was thrown in at the deep end into the hurly burly of newspaper production at the age of fourteen. I started as a copy boy – which was the bottom rung of the ladder in newspapers.

The Managing Editor then was William Haley, a large man in more than just physical size and we called him 'Big Bill'. He was a workaholic and expected his staff to be likewise, but from the copy boys upwards he was well-respected and admired.

Many a time I have known him to work all through the night. He had an old camp bed in his office to catch up on a couple of hours sleep when he worked late on a story. But behind all his bluff exterior he was a caring man and knew how to handle his staff and get the best out of them. I can recall him sending me personal Air Mail letters during the war while I was serving with the RAF in India. And this, for a very busy and important man, was a wonderful thing to do as they were handwritten, not typed out notes from his secretary.

He was later knighted and went on to become Editor of the *Times* and Director General of the BBC.

The actual Editor at this time was a Mr H.W.Archer, a quiet, unassuming man, the exact opposite of Bill Haley. He wrote a humorous column each week under the pen name of Percy Phlage as well as his brilliant leader columns.

After spending 18 months as a copy boy I was given a more permanent job, that of copy-holder to a proof-reader in the Readers' department, where all the copy was checked and corrected before going to press. A boring job to me but a completely different atmosphere from the chaos of the sub-editor's room at 3 Cross Street.

News Editors I can remember from the late 1930s up to the outbreak of war were Ted Castle, who later was married to MP Barbara Castle, John Beavan later to become Lord Ardwick and of course Frank Allaun, a great Labour man who left to work on the *Daily Herald* and then became MP for Salford.

The war then interrupted my career at the *MEN* for six years.

Bob Corfield's photograph of the Editor William Haley (in the centre) making a presentation to Rupert Denny surrounded by his staff. On the very right of the picture, seen over someone's shoulder is *Evening News* journalist Tom Jackson, who was killed in the Manchester United air crash.

The R100, created by Sir Dennis Burney who worked for Crossley Motors, is seen above the rooftops of Manchester in the early thirties. Although it was not used during the war this picture seems to epitomise the feeling of impending disaster.

FOR THE CHOICEST
FRUIT,
FLOWERS,
and VEGETABLES
SHOP ALWAYS AT
ALLENDALE LTD.
FRUITERERS and FLORISTS.
Branches throughout Manchester and District

Manchester Evening News

No. 21,941.   FRIDAY, SEPTEMBER 1, 1939   ONE PENNY.

A.R.P.
CURTAINS & BLINDS
FRYER'S of ECCLES
CHURCH ST.
Phone - - - Eccles 3325-6-7

INVASION OF POLAND BY GERMAN ARMY REPORTED

Forster to Hitler

HERR FORSTER, Nazi chief of Danzig, sent the following telegram to Hitler:—

"My Führer.—At this moment I have decreed the law enacting the reunion with the Reich. In order to make an end of the continued misery suffered by the Free City I have put into effect the following law:

1 The constitution of the Free City is suspended;

2 All legislative and executive powers lie with the chief of the State;

3 The Free City is to become part of the German Reich immediately.

4 Until the German law comes into effect the Danzig civil laws remain in force."

Hitler to Forster

Hitler telegraphed in reply:

"I accept the proclamation of the Free State of Danzig concerning the return to the German Reich.

"I thank you Gauleiter Forster and all Danzig men and women for the resolute loyalty which you and they have preserved for so many years. Greater Germany greets you with overflow in the heart. The law for reunion is ratified forthwith.

"I appoint you herewith as head of the civil administration of Danzig"

Forster to Danzig

Forster then addressed the following proclamation to the population of Danzig:

"Men and women of Danzig.— The hour for which we have longed for twenty years has come. To-day Danzig has returned to the Greater German Reich.

"The Führer has liberated us. For the first time from public buildings the Swastika flag and the German flag are flying. In the port of Danzig the flags are also flying. Church bells peal forth and we thank the Lord for our liberation. And also the Führer who has given us the opportunity to get rid of the evils of the Versailles Treaty.

"Long live a free Danzig, now returned home and long live our great Fatherland."

THE POPE MAKES NEW APPEAL

Notes Sent to Five Powers

DIPLOMATIC representatives of Britain, France, Italy, Germany, and Poland were handed an urgent appeal for peace at the Vatican.

This action had apparently only been decided upon after the Pontiff received brief reports on the international situation.

Immediately afterwards he summoned to his secretary of State, Cardinal Maglione, and Mgr. Gandolfo but as the latter was absent on his return journey from the European Powers the Cardinal asked the interested parties to call on him. Italian stanmid contained "new and very pressing insistence and from the Pope that the existing ...

WARSAW AND OTHER TOWNS ARE BOMBED

British Parliament Called for To-night

GERMAN TROOPS HAVE LAUNCHED A VIOLENT OFFENSIVE ON THE WHOLE POLISH FRONT ACCORDING TO UNCONFIRMED REPORTS. BOMBING OF POLISH TOWNS IS ALSO REPORTED

Warsaw messages say that towns attacked by German bombers include Cracow, Katowice, Czestochowa and Tczew. There are also reports of fighting at Danzig.

Warsaw and six other Polish towns were bombed by German planes. Many people have been killed and injured.

German bombers also carried out a raid on a railway station and tunnel on the Cracow-Warsaw railway line.

The official Warsaw radio later announced that Germans launched a full-scale attack against towns in the Polish Corridor and also in Upper Silesia.

Corridor towns which were being attacked were Dzialdowo and Chojnice. Fighting in Upper Silesia was in the region of Czestochowa.

Both Houses of Parliament were summoned to meet at six o'clock to-night. The Cabinet was meeting at midday, and the King was to hold a Privy Council this afternoon.

The Free City of Danzig to-day proclaimed itself part of the German Reich. Hitler sent a telegram acknowledging the reunion.

Hitler made a proclamation to his Army ordering that they " meet force with force."

A spokesman at the Polish Embassy in London said : " I have had no official news, but I heard on the wireless from Warsaw that several Polish towns, including Cracow, have been bombarded."

Later an official at the Polish Embassy confirmed the German offensive, and added : " I think the European war will start to-day. Poland will fight to the end for victory."

The Italian Embassy spokesman said the position had changed very rapidly, but added : " Quite frankly, I am still hopeful. I do still hope that something may be done."

No information was available at the German Embassy. It was said that officials were in conference.

Shipping is Warned

A blockade of the Baltic was announced by the Berlin radio, which said military measures made it necessary. Foreign shipping was warned.

A news service closely connected with the German Foreign Office accused Britain of tricking Germany during the negotiations between London and Berlin, and blamed Britain for causing the general mobilisation in Poland.

"German reports of pretended violation of German territory by Poland are pure invention, as is the Isle of the attack by Polish insurgents on Gleiwitz," it was

was issued from the White House this morning.

"The President received word by telephone at 2.52 a.m. (7.52 a.m. B.S.T.) from Mr. Biddle, the American Ambassador in Warsaw, and Mr. Bullitt, the Ambassador in Paris, that Germany has invaded Poland and that four Polish towns are being bombed.

"The President directed that all naval ships and army commands be notified by radio at once.

"There will probably be a further announcement by the State Department in a few hours."

than to meet force with force from now on. The German Army will fight the battle for the honour and the vital rights of re-born Germany with hard determination.

"I expect every soldier, mindful of the great traditions of eternal German soldiery, will ever remain conscious that he is a representative of the National Socialist Greater Germany.

"Long live our people and our Reich."

The proclamation was broadcast from the official Berlin station.

ATTACK FROM THREE DIRECTIONS

A German offensive against Poland is confirmed by information arriving in Paris.

The Germans attacked without having delivered any ultimatum, and their offensive is reported to be developing in three directions:

1. From East Prussia.
2. Towards Silesia, and
3. Northwards from Slovakia.

The Polish Embassy in Paris announced that " Germany has violated the Polish frontier at four points.

Hitler Declares "Danzig is German"

"DANZIG was and is a German city. The Corridor was and is German. All there territories owe their cluture to the German people.

Herr Hitler, facing members of the Reichstag in the Kroll Opera House, speaking into a microphone through which his speech was being relayed to the world, made this declaration to-day.

A few minutes before the meeting opened the German radio announced :—

"On a fateful day for the eGrman people the German Broadcasting Co. is relaying the meeting of the Rehstag summoned on the command of the Führer.

When Herr Hitler and Field Marshal Goering arrived all the deputies rose as they entered.

The proceedings were opened by General Goering who said: " I was able to summon you this morning at three o'clock and a large number of the members have succeeded in getting here.

100 MEMBERS WITH ARMY

"More than 100 members are not at that place where they are standing at that place where the German man would wish to stand alongside the soldiers of the German Army.

"They will do their duty as the German Reichstag will do its duty now.

"We are laying under the difficult problems of the Versailles Treaty, a problem which has become intolerable for us," began Herr Hitler.

"Without the German people the most profound barbarity would prevail there. After the world war the corridor was annexed by Poland, like many other territories.

"I HAVE TRIED PEACEFUL CHANCES

"The German minority there was the victim of numerous tortures. As always I have attempted to make many proposals for revision.

"It is a deliberate lie for anyone to suggest that we always try to bring about revisions under pressure. I have this time once more tried to pursue our demands through peaceful channels."

"All these proposals have, as you know, been refused. You know the proposals which I have made."

Hitler then recapitulated the proposals published this morning.

LOYAL AND MODEST PROPOSALS

He continued, "I have finally allowed the German proposals to be formulated and I must repeat that there is nothing more loyal and modest than these proposals. (Cheers).

"And I should like to say to the world that I alone was in the position to make such proposals. For I know very well that in making these proposals I have brought myself into opposition with millions of Germans.

"These proposals have been refused. Not only have they been answered with mobilisation but also with an increased terror against our German compatriots.

"Poland has directed its fight against Germany. It did not think of keeping its obligations to the minorities. Germany has always kept to its obligations to minorities. We have done so in every territory.

FRENCH MINORITY NOT OPPRESSED

"No Frenchman can get up and say that the FFrench minority in the Saar territory is oppressed. I have time and again uttered warnings against these development, and I have increased these warnings in the last few days.

"I have said that if the Poles oppress the minority further, and if they further try to destroy Danzig, economically and politically, Germany will no longer look on.

"I have also left no doubt that the Germany of to-day cannot be compared with the Germany of yesterday.

"They have tried to maintain that the German minority in Poland have been provocative. It is not known to me in what this 'provocation' consisted.

POLAND WAS NOT IN EARNEST

"I mask, a loss at every attempt ... it was certain that the Polish Government ... perhaps under the influence of a Jewish clique ... "

direction of peaceful solutions in Austria, and Bohemia and Moravia—all in vain.

"Two things are impossible to combine. That impossible conditions should be remedied peacefully when such peaceful remedy is the continuance of sabotage by others, and that someone who undertakes to bring about this revision would wish to use for the suffering victims of us or to the suffering victims of impossible conditions.

"It was clear that these problems had to be solved. The date for their solution, which may have been unnecessary to the Western Powers, is comprehensible to us, for that date is not unintersting to us or to the suffering victims of impossible conditions.

Discussed Problems with Poland

"I have discussed these problems and conversations with leading Polish statesmen. No one could have pretended that this was done under undue pressure.

"These proposals have been turned down, but that is not all. They were answered by mobilisation with an increasing pressure upon the German minority in Poland and a gradual attempt to throttle the life of the city of Danzig.

MOSCOW
Anglo-Soviet Pact
'Failure'

IN his speech on the ratification of the German-Soviet Pact in the Soviet Parliament, Mr. Molotov, the Soviet Premier, gave an explanation of the pact required explanations of the recent Anglo-Soviet negotiations in Moscow.

"The Anglo-Soviet proposals were unequal in the obligations imposed on Soviet Russia, he said. The negotiations lasted for four months, but obstacles proved insurmountable.

"The pact with England would have been important if a military co-operation basis was possible, but Poland refused military aid from the U.S.S.R.," he added.

HITLER'S reported order to the German Army to march and the proclamation of Forster that Danzig was pointed to the Reich caught Paris when newspapers were asserting that "French and British firmness can still save peace."

There was no official reaction.

Town's Oldest Inhabitant

From Our Radcliffe Correspondent

Oldest of Radcliffe's 30,000 inhabitants, Mrs. Charles Shasby, of 197, Ainsworth Road, will be 96 to-morrow. A native of Knutsford, she has a sister 91 and a brother 89.

When she was 12 the Crimean War was fought. A widow, Mrs. Shasby celebrated her golden wedding in 1919. Three of her six children survive, and she has seven grandchildren and ten great grandchildren.

Defence Ministers Meet

HURRIEDLY summoned by the news of Germany's attack on Poland, the Defence Ministers met at the Cabinet offices in Richmond Terrace, London, to-day.

Sir Samuel Hoare, the Home Secretary, was one of the first callers at Mr. Chamberlain at Number 10 Downing street, to-day. He arrived at 9.55 a.m., but remained only a few minutes.

About the same time the Australian and South African Commissioners went to the Dominions Office.

Eire Minister Calls

The Prime Minister's next visitors were Lord Halifax and Sir Alexander of Cadogan, who crossed over from the Foreign Office.

Madame Guilbert, a Swiss woman living at South Lambeth, London, called at No. 10 with a large bunch of flowers for Mr. and Mrs. Chamberlain.

"It is a Swiss custom to give flowers on special occasions," she said to a reporter, "and I thought I would like to do it to-day."

To-day, flowers had been placed on the bust of Lord Kitchener's statue on the base of Lord Kitchener's statue on the Horse Guards Parade beside the garden entrance to No. 10. Attached to them was a card bearing the inscription "From a private soldier. God's will be done."

Polish Envoy Calls

The Polish Ambassador arrived at No. 10 at 10.40.

Members of the Cabinet had been summoned to meet at No. 10 at 11.30, and the King is to hold a Privy Council meeting at Buckingham Palace at one o'clock.

Dr. Kordt, the German Charge d'Affaires, called at No. 10 at 10.44.

The Polish Ambassador left No. 10 after a stay of only ten minutes.

Dr. Kordt left No. 10 at 11.3.

Herr Kordt was received by the Prime Minister and Lord Halifax.

Mr. Arthur Greenwood, Deputy Leader of the Opposition, called at No. 10 at 11.5.

LANCASHIRE'S GAME OFF

Other Sporting Events Cancelled

SPORT cancelled includes the cricket at Old Trafford, where Lancashire and Surrey were in the last day of their fixture, which had previously been transferred from the Oval.

A start to the day's play had not been made.

There will be no greyhound racing at the White City. Manchester, until further notice, the enclosure having been taken over by the military authorities.

MOVING ST. DUNSTAN'S MEN

Blinded ex-soldiers of St. Dunstan's will be evacuated to-morrow under the Government's scheme from their own homes and not from the London headquarters.

AIR RAID PRECAUTIONS

Be prepared for any emergency and keep 'DETTOL,' the modern antiseptic, in your First Aid kit.

World War Two

DESPITE only two decades having passed since the 'war to end all wars', on September 3, 1939, Britain was again at war.

The *Manchester Evening News* played an important role in guiding, calming and influencing the people of Manchester. Not only was it the main means of reporting the local war effort, it was sometimes the only link with home for those serving overseas.

The *News* had given extensive coverage to the run up to the war. In 1933 the paper greeted the succession of Hitler as German Chancellor with horror, pointing out the implications of his rise to power.

The credit for giving the *News* this serious political outlook went to editor William Haley who had consistently opposed Prime Minister Chamberlain's foreign policy. In his editorial of August 25 he asked readers 'can any life be worth living in which force and not justice governs the affairs of nations and men'.

So Manchester prepared for war.

Roof spotters watch the sky over Manchester – September 1940

Preparing for war

All the top lawns and flower-beds surrounding the sunken gardens in Piccadilly, Manchester, were dug up when work began to build surface brick and concrete air-raid shelters.

Manchester men of the 8th Manchester Regiment (Ardwick) marching to the station for duty in France – 1939.

An Anderson shelter in Chorlton-cum-Hardy.

Cut out of solid rock, in the caves below Chestergate, Stockport, this ARP shelter was intended to provide accommodation for 4,000 people. It was part of a £22,000 scheme to provide bomb-proof shelter for 20,000 people. It is now a museum and tourist attraction.

The completed surface air-raid shelters in Piccadilly Gardens.

Gas masks and the great evacuation

WHAT TO TAKE

THESE are what evacuees should have when reporting for transfer to the safe areas :

SCHOOL CHILDREN

Gas mask, change of underclothing, night clothes, house shoes, spare stockings, toothbrush and comb, towel and handkerchiefs, warm coat or macintosh, and a packet of food sufficient for 24 hours.

BABIES

Dried milk for two days, 2 vests, 1 pilch, 6 napkins, 1 matinee coat, 1 pair leggings, 2 nightdresses, 1 woollen body belt, rainproof for cot, 1 pair socks, 1 shawl, safety pins, soap, towel, sponge, feeder, feeding bottle, gas mask.

TODDLERS

2 vests, 2 pairs of rompers, 3 pairs of knickers, 2 pairs of socks, shoes, or gym shoes, 2 nightdresses, and a gas mask.

MOTHERS

1 gas mask, change of clothing, 1 toothbrush, hairbrush, comb, small-tooth comb, handkerchiefs, 1 stamped addressed postcard, 1 pencil, needle, cotton, mending wool, fork, spoon, mug, plate, electric torch, and fruit and sandwiches for one day.

On September 1, 1939 the evacuation of Manchester's schoolchildren got under way. The *Manchester Evening News* attempted to convince the public of the wisdom of the measure, and of the efficiency of the process. But it was a poignant day.

The bombs did not fall on Manchester and its surrounding towns and cities immediately – but fall they did. Perhaps it was a sensible move after all to send our children to the comparative safety of the country

Children being introduced to the wearing of gas masks at St Joseph's police premises, Longsight – September, 1938.

Parents anxiously wait to see their children board the buses taking them to comparative safety outside the city centres.

It's a serious business being labelled like a parcel and packed off across the country away from your family.

Boys from Burnage High School, Manchester, calmly board a bus to take them to the station. Their gasmasks are carried in the square cardboard boxes.

Britain's first Airborne Forces trained in large numbers at Manchester's airport during World War Two.

Vampire aircraft of No.613 (City of Manchester) Squadron of the Royal Auxiliary Air Force were a familiar sight at Rignway Airport in the early years.

Designed by Roy Chadwick of AVRO, the Lancaster Bomber was the best bomber produced by any nation in World War Two. They flew from Ringway in 1941 and were made at Woodford, Chadderton, Trafford Park, Ringway, Chester and Canada.

Ft-Lt F.G.Fray briefing pilots of No.613 (City of Manchester) Squadron, Royal Auxiliary Air Force, before they left Ringway Airport for training exercises.

Soldiers and firefighters crowd round this mobile canteen which was the gift to Great Britain from the people of Trinidad and Tobago in Manchester, 1940. Note the headgear – 'cheese caps' for the soldiers and steel helmets for the fire-fighters.

A grim reminder of the consequences of war. A mobile blood transfusion unit in Piccadilly with volunteer blood donors.

A member of the Manchester Home Guard takes a risky journey across a toggle rope bridge. His partner is keeping a sharp eye-out for danger from the window of the building.

Grotesque-looking decontamination squads at work at Altrincham Gas Precautions School.

Manchester became a chief target for the German bomber planes during the war with particularly heavy raids in 1940 and 1941. A Hamburg daily newspaper reports on the success of the raid on Manchester on December 23, 1940.

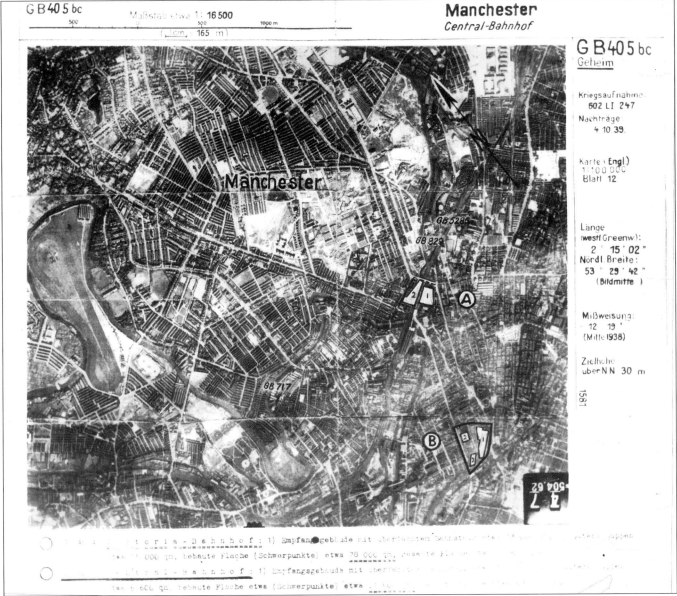

The above aerial view of Manchester, probably taken before the war, was the actual map used by the German bombers to locate key targets for their bombing raids. Victoria and Central railway stations are clearly marked A and B.

Report from the *Manchester Evening News* of the December 23 raid. The names of places and buildings are carefully vague to avoid giving the enemy too much information and, although the attack was devastating, the emphasis in the reporting is positive – 'Chins Up' – 'Blitz didn't scare them' and 'Two raiders believed down'.

The camera catches the collapse of F W Woolworth & Co store at the comer of Deansgate and St Mary's Gate, December 22, 1940.

ARP men fighting the flames at a big fire at the junction of Parker Street and Portland Street. All pictures taken during the war had to be passed by the censor and none of the photographs shown here were published at the time. It was felt to be demoralising for the public and would give the enemy too much information. Most of the censor's comments were hand written on the reverse of the picture – 'Banned by the censor' or 'Not to be published', and heavily underlined, others had an official stamp.

A dramatic view across Piccadilly Gardens of the warehouses on Parker Street.

Nearly all the photographs selected are from the same two-night blitz on December 22 and 23, 1940, but illustrate the horror and destruction of the time in the north-west. In an age when radio and newspapers were the main source of communication, scenes like this were unknown and could only be imagined – especially as the press could not communicate the true images due to censorship. The raids continued over the years until 1944, with the last major assault on the city at Christmas. All the areas around Manchester, Salford and Stockport, where key factories were sited were affected during the raids. In Oldham a V1 attack on December 24, 1944, killed 27 people.

Fire raging in Market Street and Victoria Buildings.

Flames and smoke still pour from the bombed Exchange Station on December 23, 1940. As day breaks, a lone passer-by on his way to work at one of the factories, with his gas mask over his shoulder witnesses the destruction.

Exhausted AFS and regular firemen are fighting the flames at a petroleum depot in 'a north-western town'. Despite the vague nature of the proposed caption, this picture was also banned by the censor.

A direct hit on the Manchester police headquarters.

A car burns unheeded outside Chetham's Hospital on December 23, 1940, and an unharmed tandem cycle awaits its owner.

October 1940 – Men from the emergency services survey the bomb damage as people from the neighbourhood watch at a distance.

A gaping hole torn in the nurses' home at Salford Royal Infirmary, where 14 nurses were killed during an air raid on June 2. On the right is St Philip's Church from which the Rev James Hussey was walking to comfort the wounded at the hospital when he was killed by a bomb.

Ruins at Old Shambles looking from Cannon Street towards Market Street, December 22, 1940.

Cleaning up damage that was caused during the 1940 December 'Blitz' on Manchester. Looking across Old Market Place to the Shambles.

Bleach powder being spread along the street after a bombing.

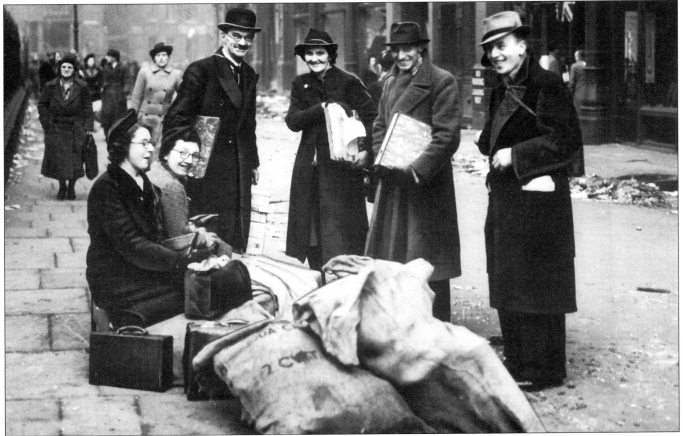

A picture which did get past the censor and was reproduced many times. It showed the fighting spirit, good humour and stubborn courage of British citizens under fire. A group of office workers with no office left in which to work.

HRH The Duke of Kent inspecting boys of the Salford Cyclist Messengers and air-raid wardens at Bexley Square, Salford, March 1941.

The Rt Hon Winston Churchill with the Chief Constable of Lancashire Sir John Maxwell inspecting the bomb damage.

King George VI and Queen Elizabeth in Manchester on February 13, 1941 at the Royal Exchange.

The grim scene on December 28, 1940, at Southern Cemetery, Manchester following the heaviest of the bombing raids in which 600 people from the cities of Manchester, Salford and Stockport died. A policeman stands on duty as friends and relatives of the dead pay their last respects.

At the end of the war in Europe, the *MEN* scored a national scoop by being the first paper to publish the great news. Realising that the end of the war was in sight, the managing editor prepared an up-to-the-minute edition every night with the giant headline 'War is Over'. When at last the news agency 'flash' came of the Nazi capitulation on May 7, 1945, everything was ready. Within minutes, ahead of the whole country, the paper was on the streets with the news everyone had waited so long to hear. Crowds outside the *MEN* office eagerly scanned the papers announcing the end of the war in Europe. Here, civilians mix with those from the forces to celebrate the news.

VICTORY SPECIAL

Manchester Evening News

№3,701   MONDAY, MAY 7, 1945   Three Halfpence

WAR IN EUROPE ENDED TO-DAY

Doenitz Orders "All Germans Surrender"

TERMS SIGNED AT RHEIMS H.Q. OF GEN. EISENHOWER

"GOEBBELS' BODY FOUND IN BERLIN"

GOEBBELS'S body and those of his family have been found in an air-raid shelter near the Berlin Reichstag, according to unconfirmed reports reaching Moscow.

Many explanations have been offered to account for the disappearance of Goebbels. One of the latest, which fits in with the report of the finding of his body, is that he perished in a suicide pact with his wife and his entire family.

The Text in Full

ALL THE GERMAN FORCES HAVE SURRENDERED AND THE WAR IN EUROPE IS OVER!

It came to an end this afternoon with an announcement of total German surrender and complete Allied Victory made over the Flensburg Radio by Count von Krosigk, German Foreign Minister.

Count Krosigk was making the announcement on behalf of Admiral Doenitz, the new Führer of what is left of Germany.

The surrender was made unconditionally to the Western Allies and Russia at 2 41 a.m. (French time) to-day in the big Rheims schoolhouse which is General Dwight Eisenhower's headquarters. It was signed for Germany by Colonel - General Gustav Jodl, the new Chief of Staff of the Wermacht.

The surrender was signed for General Eisenhower by Lieut.-General Bedwell-Smith, Chief of Staff. It was also signed by General Susloparoff for Russia, and General Sevez for France.

An official Allied announcement of the surrender was then made from Rheims. Eisenhower had not been present at the signing, but he received Jodl and General-Admiral Friedburg immediately afterwards.

After signing the full surrender General Jodl was given permission to speak. "With this signature," he said, "the German people and Armed Forces are for better or worse delivered into the victors' hands."

The German-controlled Prague radio later denied the unconditional surrender report broadcast by Flensburg as far as Russia was concerned. "Only the fight against the Western Allies has ceased," said the radio.

"We Succumb"

Count von Krosigk said the surrender was ordered by Admiral Doenitz, and added : " After a heroic fight of almost six years of incomparable hardness Germany has succumbed to the overwhelming power of her enemies."

He added that to continue the war would only mean senseless bloodshed, and the collapse of all German forces had made it imperative to demand the end of hostilities.

Krosigk added : "We must accept this burden and stand loyally by our obligations. From the collapse let us save one thing—unity. No one must be under any illusions about the severity of the terms. We must face our fate."

All preparations had been made to-day for Mr. Churchill to announce the German surrender from No. 10, Downing-street.

It has been necessary to arrange the simultaneous announcement in all the Allied capitals, but the first flash of victory was all that was necessary to enable the Premier to release the news.

Balcony Hope

It was generally hoped that Mr. Churchill would at the end of this announcement address the crowd from the balcony at No. 10.

It was known that announcement by Mr. Churchill over the radio this evening would be followed by a broadcast by the King at nine o'clock.

Mr. Churchill's full-scale broadcast will come on Thursday, May 10, the fifth anniversary of his appointment as Prime Minister.

Mr. Churchill will also announce the end of the European War in the Commons, but he will make no lengthy speech. After party leaders have added their few words the Speaker will lead M.P.s to St. Margaret's, Westminster, for a service of thanksgiving.

How News Reached the Crowds

THIS country first learned the news of the full German surrender from the Stop Press announcements in the evening papers, and then by a B.B.C. announcement at 3 p.m.

The B.B.C. said: "Here in London there is growing expectation that Mr. Churchill will broadcast to the nation in a matter of Lours.

"The actual time of his victory announcement may depend on telephone talks that have been going on between London, Washington, and Moscow."

Listeners to the B.B.C. were reminded to-day that the King will broadcast at 9 p.m. on the day Mr. Churchill announces the end of the war in Europe.

Crowds of people thronged Whitehall waiting for the expected announcement and a painter was busy completing a notice in yellow paint containing three words—' War against Japan."

V(E)-Day's Court Cases Adjourned

All summonses due for hearing at Salford Magistrates' Court on V(E)-Day and V(E)-Day Plus One will be automatically adjourned a week and all persons due to appear on bail will have their bail extended for a week.

The court will sit as usual to deal with overnight prisoners, and will also deal with any case if especially asked to.

"Lord Haw-Haw" Not in Dublin

Reports that "Lord Haw-Haw" was one of the occupants of the German plane which landed at Gormanstown, near Dublin, on Saturday, are untrue.

THE GREAT DAY

TATTOO

British Push South From Rangoon

British troops, leaving units to mop-up in Rangoon, are pushing south from the city in heavy pre-monsoon rains.

In the oil regions Yenanama, 27 miles south of Minbu, has fallen.—Reuter.

No News Of King Leopold

Government officials in Brussels said to-day that they had no further news concerning King Leopold.

Court circles have received these tidings with some disquietude.

THE POLICE STAND BY—JUST IN CASE

METROPOLITAN policemen were standing by to-day, in readiness for the expected announcement that the war had ended and called with the crowds of revellers expected to converge in the West End.

Service police of all the Allies were also ready for their patrols. The civil police pool consisted of hundreds of men who can be rushed to any spot where the situation might show signs of getting out of hand.

The police will take drastic action against revellers only if they attempt to damage public or private property, and will look with a fatherly eye on anyone who celebrates too much.

Only if a person is incapable or unruly will he be taken into "protective custody."

No special arrangements have been made for controlling the crowds in Manchester I was told at police headquarters to-day.

"We are always able to call out more police in an emergency," said an official.

The Forties

After the war was over...

Victory over Japan, VJ Day, August 15, 1945. The dropping of the atomic bomb on Hiroshima and Nagasaki brought the end to World War Two. Four ladies from Higher Openshaw found their wartime holiday in Blackpool had become a peace celebration.

More celebrations and the demand for fireworks, even after six years of gunfire, bomb explosions, landmines and V-rockets was as great as ever. People queue for whatever fireworks were available at this Urmston shop.

The City Police band play in Albert Square to a small, damp, but happy crowd. Round the Albert Memorial a large hoarding announces a Manchester and District Exhibition to plan and rebuild the city.

On May 23, 1945 the Coalition Government which had brought the war in Europe to a successful conclusion came to an end. The General Election was set for July 5 with the counting of votes delayed until July 26 so that the Service votes could be added. The result was a landslide for Labour. This amazing picture above and the close up of the car below were taken on June 25, 1945, during Winston Churchill's campaign. His motorcade is actually crossing Mosley Street from York Street and almost completely swamped by the crowd which packed both Mosley Street and overflowed on to the area of devastation now occupied by Piccadilly Plaza.

Manchester Evening News

LATE NIGHT FINAL

ROYAL WEDDING SOUVENIR

THURSDAY, NOV. 20, 1947. 24,466. Three Halfpence.

Cheering Crowd Breaks into Palace Courtyard

WORLD HEARS RADIANT PRINCESS SAY "I WILL"

OVER 2,000 CASUALTIES

MILLIONS throughout the world, listening by their radio sets, heard to-day the shy, whispered "I will" of Princess Elizabeth as the Archbishop of Canterbury asked her in the golden blaze of Westminster Abbey: "Elizabeth Alexandra Mary, wilt thou take this man to thy wedded husband?"

The deep, confident tone of her bridegroom, the Duke of Edinburgh, contrasted to the quiet responses of the Princess, but both were clearly heard in the Abbey and by the vast unseen audience. The Duke was addressed simply as "Philip."

Phrase by phrase the bridegroom repeated after the Archbishop the declaration plighting troth "to love and to cherish." Momentarily their hands were unclasped.

Then they were rejoined, with this difference, that the Princess was holding her bridegroom's hand.

The beaming Archbishop, with the words "with this ring I thee wed," brought to life a sound picture of the scene.

The scene was an unforgettable one for the congregation of 2500—Kings and Queens, soldiers in khaki, admirals in blue and gold, choir boys in white and scarlet, the children of the Chapels Royal in their robes, Indian Princes in their turbans, and Ambassadors with multi-coloured ribbons of foreign orders slashed across their breasts.

Sparkling Fanfare of Trumpets

They had watched breathlessly as the brilliant ceremony began. At the West door the bride was joined by her eight bridesmaids and the two pages. Trumpeters in blue and gold uniforms sounded a sparkling fanfare as she walked slowly through the great Gothic door.

It was obvious that the two little pages—Prince William of Gloucester and Prince Michael of Kent—in tartan kilts, were having great difficulty with her train.

The bridegroom repeatedly looked back to see how the pages were managing, and to help them he deliberately slowed the pace of his bride and himself. The King, standing on his daughter's left as she moved to the altar, stooped down to grasp the train for a few moments and so help the pages.

Leaning on her father's arm with her pages and bridesmaids following and preceded by singing choirboys in white and scarlet, she walked in procession along the six-feet wide crimson carpet laid along the whole length of nave and choir. Then the Duke joined her at the foot of the sanctuary steps. They smiled at each other.

Bride and bridegroom were together in the centre of a group of four, with the King on his daughter's left and the best man on the bridegroom's right.

The Dean of Westminster (Dr. Alan Don) in cope of cloth of gold read the exhortation from the Prayer Book: "Dearly beloved we are gathered together here in the sight of God."

Then the Archbishop of Canterbury (Dr. G. F. Fisher), in mitre and cope of white and gold brocade, performed the actual marriage service.

"I will," declared the bridegroom. The words were repeated later by the Princess.

"I will," she said softly, when the Archbishop asked her, "Elizabeth Alexandra Mary, wilt thou have this man to thy wedded husband?"

The Duke placed a ring of Welsh gold on the Princess's wedding finger. Then came blessings from the Archbishop on bride and bridegroom, accompanied by Princess Margaret and the two pages, went up the sanctuary steps to kneel at the high altar, and the King moved to his seat in the sanctuary beside the Queen.

Register Signed in the Chapel

At the singing ended, bride and bridegroom, the King and Queen, Queen Mary, Princess Margaret, Princess Andrew of Greece, and the two pages, with the Archbishop of Canterbury, and the Precentor of the Abbey (the Rev C. Armitage) in the rear left the sanctuary by a door at the side of the altar and went into the Chapel of Edward the Confessor for the signing of the register and other books kept at the Abbey for such royal occasions.

A third and final fanfare from the trumpeters announced that the signing had been completed. With the organ thundering out the stirring chords of Mendelssohn's Wedding March the newly-married Princess and her sailor husband walked slowly through choir and nave to the west door.

As the bridal pair passed the King and Queen, the bridegroom bowed, and Princess Elizabeth dropped a deep curtsy. One of the pages fell over in the Abbey as the bridal procession made its way to the vestry.

The Abbey bells rang out as Princess Elizabeth and her husband walked towards the West door of the Abbey. The Prince, smiling happily, waved to the cheering multitudes as followed by her husband she entered the Glass Coach and drove back to the Palace, acclaimed wildly all the way.

As Princess Elizabeth Duchess of Edinburgh and her husband returned to the Palace waving, saluting, and smiling, she was looking even happier than when she left. Both were

(Turn to Back Page)

Picture the World Has Waited For
THE HAPPY COUPLE

HERE is the happiest picture of the great occasion—the picture that every married couple, of whatever estate, treasures most. The ceremony is over, and now the happy couple leave together hand-in-hand.

—Pages 2 and 3:—
FULL DESCRIPTION
Pages 4, 5 and Back Page:
PHOTOGRAPHS

City Sends Its Greetings

ALDERMAN MISS MARY KINGSMILL JONES, Lord Mayor of Manchester, sent this telegram to Princess Elizabeth: "On this joyful occasion citizens of Manchester send to Your Royal Highness a loyal and heartfelt message of deep affection and wish for Your Royal Highness and His Royal Highness the Duke of Edinburgh all possible happiness for long years to come."

A special *MEN* edition of November 20, 1947, which celebrated the wedding of Princess Elizabeth to the Duke of Edinburgh.

Two years after their marriage, on March 30, 1949, the Princess, accompanied by her husband the Duke of Edinburgh is being conducted on an inspection of the guard of honour of the Eighth Ardwick Battalion (Manchester Regiment) TA by Lieutenant Colonel R.D.Martin-Bird in Albert Square, Manchester. In the background is the Duke of Edinburgh.

The same day Princess Elizabeth visited New Cross flats, Hulme, Manchester where she was presented with a bouquet of flowers by Elsie Paine. The Princess was shown round one of the flats and when she came out she was smiling. When the Lord Mayor Dame Mary Kingsmill-Jones asked if something had amused her, the Princess replied that the old lady had called her 'luv' – a northern term of endearment.

In 1949 the last of the old trams was seen on the streets of Manchester.

… and here are the crews who had served on the No.1007.

The Fifties

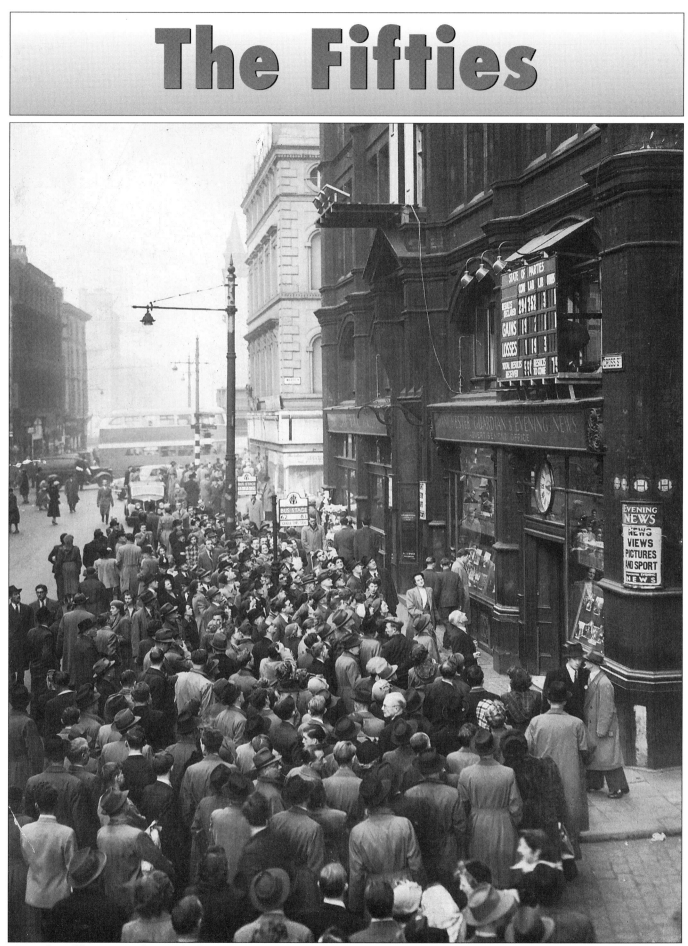

Crowds milling around outside the *Manchester Evening News* office to see the latest election results on October 25, 1951. The Conservatives won the election by a small majority.

The London newspaper strike, March, 1955. With no newspapers in London for six days in succession, the provincial papers were in great demand, and here we see a queue of people outside the Fleet Street office of the *Manchester Guardian* and the *Manchester Evening News* waiting to buy a paper.

From the mid-fifties to the early sixties there was considerable unrest at Manchester Docks which resulted in a number of strikes. Dockers here are voting to take strike action.

Strike pickets wait outside the dock gates during the 1957 strike in Manchester.

A lone policemen stands watch on Manchester's deserted dockside.

Sentinel cranes, 'frozen' by a protest strike, mark the silent skyline beyond during one of the fifties dockyard strikes.

While the country's shipbuilding yards lie silent, all is bustle and normal activity in the Manchester docks during the 1957 strike. This picture shows No.9 dock where ships are busy loading, unloading and accepting freight. The only part of the Manchester docks affected by the great strike is the dry dock.

Merchant ships move up and down the Ship Canal as usual, helping to keep the country's exports flowing.

Britain's first-ever bomber, the historic Avro 504 Biplane, was rebuilt by four veteran craftsmen who had worked on the original 504 production lines during World War One. The biplane was built specially to take part in the film of the life of legless fighter ace Group Captain Douglas Bader who learned to fly in an Avro 504.

A Lancaster bomber, brought out of storage for the Associated British Picture Corporation's film *The Dambusters* starring Richard Todd as Guy Gibson VC, and Michael Redgrave as Dr Barnes Wallis, the man who invented the bombs which blew the dams in Germany during World War Two.

You never know who you might meet in Manchester. In 1958 Cary Grant chats to a student in St Peter's Square during his surprise tour of the city prior to a personal appearance at the Theatre Royal.

Sweeping St Leonard's Street in readiness for one of the many parties which took place in Manchester to celebrate the Coronation of Queen Elizabeth on June 2, 1953.

The world's first successful stored-programme computer was another Manchester University first and built by professors Fred Williams and Tom Kilburn, aided by engineer Geoff Toothill. It ran its first programme in 1948 with a memory capacity of 32 words, but until this breakthrough computers had been just calculating machines.

1958 and the famous picture of Jodrell Bank in Cheshire by Tom Stuttard at the time of the first moon landing by the Russian Sputnik 1. Jodrell Bank, now a popular tourist attraction, was the creation of Professor Sir Bernard Lovell of Manchester University.

September 8, 1957, and the fire at Pauldens Department Store which completely gutted this famous retail outlet in Stretford Road, All Saints. The fire began on the first floor in the early evening and in less that three hours the building was completely gutted. More than 20 fire-fighting appliances were at the scene. The remains are seen here still smouldering the following day.

...and a fast forward to 1969 with this dramatic picture of a double-decker bus which had crashed through the road at the site of the Pauldens fire.

Disaster at Wythenshawe

On March 14, 1957, a BEA airliner crashed into houses at the end of the runway at Manchester's Ringway airport. Squads of firemen toiled over red-hot brickwork and smouldering timber in the search for a woman and child missing in one of the houses. All 20 occupants of the plane – 15 passengers and five crew – plus the Wythenshawe woman and her son died in the crash. The plane, flagship of the Discovery class of Viscounts, was on flight from Amsterdam and overshot the runway while coming in to land. The appalling disaster highlighted the concern of all residents living in close proximity to the airport.

The end of the runway after the Viscount air disaster in Wythenshawe in 1957. Smoke still obscures the houses demolished by the aircraft as the rescue operation continues and officials in the foreground search the ground for clues to the crash.

Manchester United party pictured as they left Ringway Airport on the ill-fated airliner which crashed at Munich. From the left: Jackie Blanchflower, Bill Foulkes, Walter Crickmer secretary, *Manchester Guardian* journalist Don Davies, Roger Byrne captain, Duncan Edwards, Albert Scanlon, Frank Swift, Ray Wood, Dennis Viollet, journalist Archie Ledbrook, Jeff Bent, Mark Jones, journalist Alf Clarke.

The victims of Munich

DAVID MEEK, former United reporter, was a young journalist at the time of the Munich crash.

A LARGE part of Manchester eats, sleeps and talks sport, especially football, and in particular Manchester United and Manchester City.

It's why the sports department of the *Manchester Evening News* makes soccer a priority with four specialist reporters concentrating on the clubs in the area of Greater Manchester.

Paul Hince followed Peter Gardner as the man writing about Manchester City while I count it my good fortune to have been the Manchester United correspondent more than 35 years.

As you might gather from that length of stint, it is not a job you easily walk away from, and I am not alone in that respect. My predecessor, the much-respected and well-liked Tom Jackson, had represented the paper at Old Trafford for 25 years before becoming one of the eight journalists killed in the Munich air crash of 1958.

Indeed, looking back through the archives it might well be that there have only been four regular correspondents specialising in Manchester United since the club was formed in 1878. The

Manchester Evening News has long recognised the importance of United and City in the hearts of its readers which is why in 1958 they switched their leader writer from politics to sport to cover the tragedy of Munich.

Manchester virtually came to a stop when the news of the terrible accident at Munich reached the city. The first flashes were wired into the *Evening News* offices and the Editor, Tom Henry, immediately produced a special edition.

People waited outside the office for the latest reports as word spread of the worst tragedy in the history of English football as the team were flying home after a European Cup-tie against Red Star Belgrade and made a refuelling stop at Munich.

It was an anguished way to start a career as Manchester United correspondent. It was also meant to be a temporary appointment, but there never seems to have been sufficient of a lull in the flow of news from Old Trafford to consider my assignment completed.

The ill-fated Elizabethan airliner in flames at Munich.

Bill Foulkes, one of the few survivors, is pictured amidst the wreckage at the scene of the crash.

A spectacular collapse of Barton Bridge during its construction in 1959. Officials survey the damage before the canal below can be re-opened.

Belle Vue… and after the great fire of 1958 this is all that remained of the York Restaurant and the popular Coronation Ballroom.

The Sixties

The world's longest-running peak time drama series was started by Granada Television on December 9, 1960. Who was to guess that the homely scenes from Manchester and Salford would be viewed all over the world? Here, in the back room of the Rover's Return – the 'snug' - Minnie Caldwell gets another telling off from Ena Sharples while Martha Longhurst concentrates on her milk stout. The landlord, Jack Walker, looks on.

Another popular character in *Coronation Street*, Elsie Tanner (centre) at her marriage to Steve, a US airman, surrounded by friends and neighbours from the series.

On this page you can see the sequence of events following the derailment and crash of a school excursion train carrying nearly 250 children from Staffordshire to York. The accident happened at Cheadle Hulme station and these are a few of the contact prints from a cameraman at the scene of the crash. The picture editor would select one or more photographs to illustrate the reporter's copy, and you can see in the front page opposite how the contact picture in the middle of the first and third rows have been used to fit the page layout.

In 1965 one of the world's most famous infants, the original Rolls-Royce Silver Ghost came back to its birthplace. The visit to Royce Court, Hulme was, for the unveiling of a plaque recording that nearby stood the first Rolls-Royce factory where it was built in 1906.

Silent demonstrations... holding posters, off-duty firemen from all over the North-West massed outside Manchester town hall while their pay claim was discussed.

The scene in Moult Street on October 30, 1969, when a serious fire broke out in the foundry of the *Manchester Evening News*. Two of the 24 firemen tackling the outbreak were overcome by fumes and had to be treated at Manchester Royal Infirmary.

Children playing
unsupervised on
the cobbled street
of these terraced
houses. Rocking
horses, dressing
up, dolls and
prams are still
among the toys
and games of
children today!

A housewife
'stoning' the steps
was a
commonplace sight
in the old terraced
streets of
Manchester – even
in the sixties.

A missing child – the horror of all parents – but this story had a happy ending. After an all night search this little boy was found trapped in a Hulme communal flats dustbin. Covered in ashes the frightened boy is carried into his home by his dad, with his anxious mum and police officer who conducted the search close behind.

Back to the News...

TOM WAGHORN – Feature writer, former chief sub-editor, remembers Cross Street and Tom Henry who was Editor from 1946-1968.

EDITOR Tom Henry loved to hire his staff in unusual circumstances. In the early sixties I was on a Scottish climbing holiday and received a telegram: 'Phone immediately. Reverse charges – Henry.'

Within seven days, not having even applied for a job and with three weeks' holiday unused, I was Postbag editor. Cross Street then had an extension, the Dilworth Building, which was reached by a covered-in bridge. I shared a room 'down the Dilworth' with John Alldridge, our star writer, city councillor, occasional *Coronation Street* scriptwriter and producer for Withington Players.

The swinging sixties they might have been in London, but the *Evening News* in those days ran on brown ale, black type and hot lead. Tom Henry ran his paper like an ironmaster, growling commands at his middle-aged executives who in turn snapped at the young reporters and subs who yelled at the humble copy-boys who ran the reporters' stories, sheet by sheet, to the chief sub-editor.

The boys crouched at the messengers' desk, this platoon of teenage runners, in the gloomiest corner of the editorial floor, making thick black tea in chipped mugs and leaping like scalded cats when some harassed hack shouted "Boy!"

We still have these messengers even in the late nineties, girls as well as boys, but as the hot lead has now been replaced by modern computer typesetting.

I think Tom Henry would have approved!

On the stone! Overseers and sub-editors look on anxiously as Tom Henry, on the right, makes a last check of the front page before going to press. Tom Henry, one of the newspaper's most respected editors, died in April 1983, aged 73.

A reel of paper is sent through the tunnel on the steel conveyor belt.

In the machine room, a heavy metal page is fitted to the huge presses.

The cramped hot and dangerous conditions of the machine room as the presses roll and the first editions comes off the press.

How the *News* reached its readers

Motor vans gradually replaced the pony and trap. *Manchester Evening News* Morris vans line up in Warren Street opposite the Old Thatched House pub.

A 1956 van carried a 'bushing' machine, which could add the latest Stop Press news and results to the papers. They were particularly useful for football matches – and the modern, distinctive yellow and black 'mobiles' were used in the same way until recently.

Two delivery vans in 1971 wait outside the old Stockport Branch Office on Shaw Heath.

This picture shows the classified room at Cross Street in the fifties. Small ads are the lifeblood of any evening newspaper and are an ideal marketplace for anything from children's bicycles to cars or houses and jobs.

The van carrying the bushing maching in operation outside Manchester United football ground.

Left: A photographer finds a good spot to cover the Whitsuntide Walk.

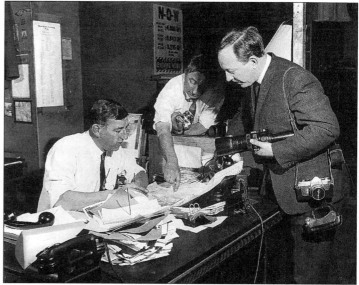

Above: MEN photographers Stan Royle and John Featherstone check the map with Picture Editor Jack Abel before shooting off on another assignment.

Below: Sports desk at Cross Street in 1967. On the left of our picture is David Meek, Manchester United reporter, on his left is Neville Bolton, our current Sports Editor. On the right of the picture (opposite Neville) is Vernon Addison who was the Sports Editor of the day, and on his right is George Dowson who now covers Rugby League.

Goodbye Cross Street

The mammoth operation moving from Cross Street to Deansgate in August 1970 was a far-sighted idea to share the resources of one publishing plant at Northcliffe House on Deansgate. The new buildings adjacent held the editorial, advertising and commercial offices of *The Guardian, Daily Mail, Sunday People* and ourselves. No newspapers were in direct opposition and it meant that the presses were used night and day.

These two pictures show the heavy Linotype machines being taken out and tied securely to a transporter for the short journey to Deansgate.

Hello Deansgate

Settled in its new home, the first Deansgate printed copies of the *Manchester Evening News* are anxiously scanned by Ken Searle *MEN* Managing Director on the left, Andy Harvie, later Managing Director, who was in charge of the move, Hirst Adams from the firm of architects, Leach, Rhodes and Walker, and Max Hallas, from Associated Newspapers.

The whole move was made within 24 hours from the final edition of the Pink Sports paper being printed at Cross Street on Saturday, to the *Guardian* being printed at Deansgate on the Sunday evening so that no editions of either paper were lost.

Brian Redhead – Previously Northern Editor of the *Guardian*, Brian became Editor of the *News* in 1969 and left in 1975. He later became senior presenter of the BBC's *Today* programme, but remained a great supporter of Manchester. He died in January 1994, aged 64.

Doug Emmett – From his position as Assistant Editor, Doug took over as Editor and supervised the change from broadsheet to a tabloid newspaper in 1983. He retired in November of that year but sadly died in July 1988.

Above: Brian Redhead, the Editor, in 1971 and Tom Henry, former Editor of the *Manchester Evening News*, survey the new stainless steel statue of *Vigilance* in Spinningfield, designed by Keith Godwin head of the School of Sculpture, Manchester Polytechnic, Faculty of Art and Design.

Bob Corfield, photographer in the centre surrounded by his colleagues, is seen at his retirement presentation after 50 years at the *Manchester Evening News*.

The Seventies

The Osmond Brothers at the Free Trade Hall in the early seventies. Fourteen-year-old Donny Osmond sings to screaming weeny boppers who came in their hundreds to worship their new idols.

Ecstatic fans at a Bay City Rollers concert held at Belle Vue, Manchester in 1975.

Scammonden Bridge – M62 1969, and just taking shape high up on the Pennine moors is a bridge which would span the 600ft gap left by blasting a route for the Lancashire-Yorkshire motorway through the wall of the Scammonden Valley. The M62 motorway was opened in 1971.

The Robin Hood railway bridge under construction at Clifton, Salford.

The M62 has proved to be a valuable link over the Pennines, except when everyone wants to use it at once! The motorway police arrive to try to sort out this hold-up in the Irwell Valley section in 1978.

Another view of the bridge being built over the River Irwell at Clifton.

The mighty Wurlitzer organ that had entertained thousands at the Odeon Cinema is moved out of the theatre by volunteers for the Lancastrian Theatre Organ Trust. It was to be re-assembled and situated in the Free Trade Hall.

In January 1973 Earl Mountbatten attends Indian Association celebrations in Rochdale and meets Cyril Smith, MP.

Danny Kaye, the uncrowned king of entertainers, held court in a Manchester hotel in 1974 prior to conducting the Hallé Orchestra at the Free Trade Hall. The visit fulfilled a promise made 15 years previously to Sir John Barbirolli that he would one day conduct the orchestra in Manchester. His 12,000 mile round trip from California was arranged by the Variety Club of Great Britain, with the aim to raise money for handicapped and under-privileged children in the North-West.

July 26, 1978 and gynaecologist Mr Patrick Steptoe (nearest the camera) and scientist Dr Robert Edwards talk to the world's press after the birth of the first test tube baby by caesarean section at Oldham General Hospital. The birth followed 12 years of research by Dr Edwards and his team at Cambridge University in consultation with Dr Steptoe at Oldham.

1977 and a new Speakers' Corner outside the Library in St Peter's Square. Here, this speaker with his assistant dressed in Pilgrim's costume is against Britain joining the European Common Market.

This shows the redevelopment in the Market Street area in Manchester and the site of the Arndale Centre.

A photograph by Bill Bachelor of the Wellington Inn and Sinclair's Oyster Rooms together known as the Old Shambles. They were saved from demolition during the new development in an amazing building operation in 1971. The entire building was raised 4ft 9½in from its original street level to fit in with the new surrounding buildings. The Wellington Inn had survived for over 600 years and, as we saw earlier, had even escaped Hitler's bombs.

131

In 1975 public opinion won against Greater Manchester Council who wanted to turn Sackville Gardens into a construction site for the planned Picc-Vic underground rail link. The Picc-Vic idea was scrapped and later replaced by Metrolink.

The Eighties

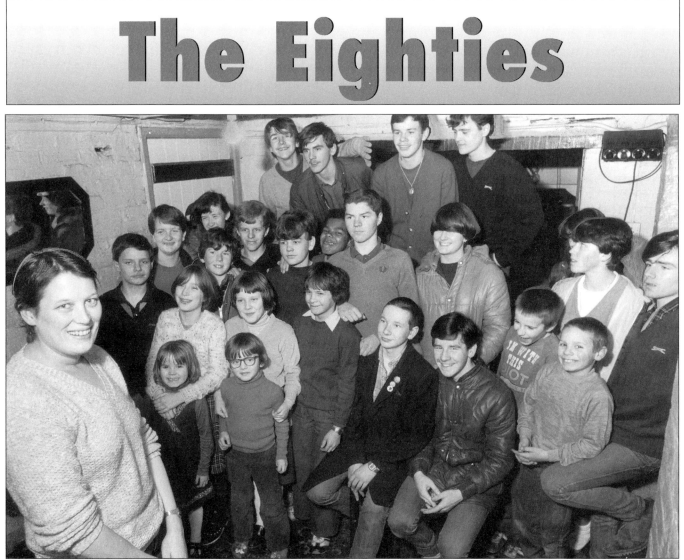

In 1981 Maggie and Chris Nolan with the help of local youngsters turned their cellar into a youth club for the children of the Collyhurst area.

Residents of Miriam Street, Bradshaw Avenue and Gail Close of Failsworth were dancing in the street when they were voted the best decorated neighbourhood for the Royal Wedding of Prince Charles and Lady Diana Spencer in July 1981.

Making a grab for cakes in Coppice Close, Woodley these youngsters celebrate the wedding with another street party.

Council plans £½m lights, song and dance extravaganza

Super city Christmas!

Massive festive campaign to woo back the shoppers

By GERALD BROWN

MANCHESTER is set to transform itself into a magical wonderland this Christmas.

The city centre will become a riot of festive lights and tableaux in a £500,000 extravaganza, plus buskers, open-air singing and even the possibility of a traditional Chinese dragon dance.

It's all part of a long-term campaign by the city council and big business to lure thousands of shoppers back to the city.

There has been concern that over the 5 years, Manchester has slipped from [...] as leading trading [...]

Maxine Burns, Christine Summerfield and Barbara Heatchcote of A H Knowles, P R, of Manchester, showing a display of goods which will be on sale to promote the city.

1982 and the city gets set for a bumper Christmas with specially illuminated streets and activities.

Rain dampened the colourful spectacle of a pony parade through the city centre which was part of the magical World of Christmas events. Children in fancy dress were led in a parade by a coach bearing the Lord Mayor and Lady Mayoress and a sleigh carrying Father Christmas. However, crowds were happy to turn out with umbrellas in Market Street to see them.

Pope comes to Heaton Park

A smile and a blessing from Pope John Paul II who arrived for a historic visit to the North-West in 1982.

Crowds turn out in their thousands at Heaton Park, to await the arrival of the Pope, hoping he will see their messages.

To a rapturous welcome, the Pope tours Heaton Park, Manchester in his Leyland built Pope-mobile greeting the people, some of whom had camped overnight to see him in June 1982.

centaur
Fine British Clothes for Men
CENTAUR CLOTHES LTD LEEDS LS1 3BS

A FRIEND DROPPING IN

FIRST EXTRA

Manchester Evening News

35,134 — FRIDAY, APRIL 30, 1982 — 14p

PLOUGHMANS LUNCH AND LICENSED BAR CONTINENTAL RESTAURANT 1st Floor at Lewis's

TWENTY-FOUR HOUR TV & RADIO GUIDE — PAGE 11

BRITAIN'S BIGGEST REGIONAL EVENING NEWSPAPER

Commando chief in flying visit to fleet

THE chief of Britain's commando forces, Major-General Jeremy Moore, has paid a flying visit to the Falkland Islands fleet in the South Atlantic.

Gen Moore conferred on Fearless (right) with Brig Julian Thompson, commander of the fleet's 3,000 assault troops, and Commodore Michael Clapp, the Navy's chief of amphibious warfare.

Fearless is the command ship from which the main body of troops could be flung at the beaches if Britain tries to retake the Falklands.

Argentine cuts mail links with Britain

ARGENTINA today cut off mail and telegraph communications with Britain, although telephone and Telex ties continued.

The government in Buenos Aires also said the joint chiefs would assume "control" over all foreign news published or broadcast in Argentina, but without direct censorship.

The directives were not totally clear, and the government told media executives: "If you have any doubt consult the joint chiefs."

Only official communiques from the nation's ruling junta were considered as reliable news about Argentine logistical movement in the conflict zone.

Although Argentina's 27 million people are reported to be almost unanimously behind the recapture of the Falklands and have supported the government with enthusiastic mass patriotic rallies, an isolated few are beginning to question whether a war would be worth the price.

"We don't have money to spend on adventures like this," said a retired merchant seaman. "Argentina has plenty of land on the continent."

Radio broadcasts presumably produced by the authorities but not specifically identified are warning Argentines not to commit "seditious acts."

FLASHPOINT!

Time's up—but still trying

By A SPECIAL CORRESPONDENT

THE FALKLANDS crisis is now at flashpoint. Forces of both sides are poised to attack unless diplomacy pays off at the last minute.

A total British blockade went into force at noon. Any planes and ships which come within 200 miles of the Argentine-occupied islands will be liable to attack by the powerful task force now assembled in the area.

And Britain has made it plain that this is no bluff.

The Buenos Aires decision to establish its own 200-mile "no-go" zone around the Falklands, as well as South Georgia, the Sandwich Isalnds and the Argentine mainland, means that bloody conflict could be only hours away.

Any British ship or plane found inside the zone would be regarded as hostile and "treated accordingly", said the three-man ruling junta.

The zone would operate "as of today" — apparently meaning immediately.

Meanwhile the desperate peace efforts by America and the United Nations continue without pause.

Fleet's ice-cool hero: Page 17

Although Argentina has told Washington that its latest proposals are "unsatisfactory" and require further clarification, US Vice-President George Bush today said that Secretary of State Alexander Haig is "going the extra mile" to find a diplomatic solution.

And this afternoon Argentina's foreign minister Costa Mendez was due to meet United Nations Secretary General Javier Perez de Cuellar.

Diplomatic sources said the UN has "contingency plans" to act as intermediary and place an international "presence" on the islands, which Argentina occupied four weeks ago after 149 years of British rule.

But there were no indications so far of an understanding under which both Britain and Argentina would accept a peace-making role by the UN.

COSTA MENDEZ
Meeting at UN

PEREZ DE CUELLAR
Peace in his hands?

Mr Costa Mendez was expected to discuss all possible options. These include the appointment of a UN administrator or caretaker with a small administrative group which would be placed on the islands pending a diplomatic settlement.

Support

Washington administration sources said the United States might issue a statement in support of Britain if the crisis erupts into a military conflict.

And Vice-President Bush said: "I reiterate our fundamental support and the fundamental importance we place on our relationship with the United Kingdom, but I cannot comment further as long as we're trying to play a useful role."

Earlier, the US Senate approved a pro-British resolution calling on Argentina to remove its troops from the Falklands.

The House of Representatives foreign affairs committee expressed "full US diplomatic support" for Britain should she go to war with Argentina.

Mr Haig was ready to fly to Buenos Aires or London at the slightest hint that it might achieve something.

Argentina's decision to impose its own air-sea exclusion zone is seen in London as having a number of objectives.

It would raise morale for the estimated 10,000 Argentine troops on the Falklands.

It could be a blatant spinning out by the junta of negotiations to gain time to strengthen its forces.

It might also allow negotiations to restart, possibly through the United Nations, without giving the impression that Argentina had been humiliated by Britain.

But the critical question was whether Argentina would attempt to supply its troops on the islands after Britain's noon deadline.

Morale

Rumours in Buenos Aires that the junta might seek a pre-emptive strike against the task force were believed to be an attempt to keep Britain guessing.

It was accepted that Argentina had embarked on a high-risk strategy. If its aircraft carrier was sunk its whole fleet would be seriously damaged.

There was nothing in the latest Argentine communique to indicate what military action it would take against the British task force.

When a foreign reporter asked retired Admiral Jorge Fraga at a Press conference if the Argentine navy was at a disadvantage because it has British-made ships and missiles familiar to the enemy, he said: "No. For the same reason we are familiar with what they have."

At Westminster it is felt that Mrs Thatcher and her advisers will now have to calculate how far British public opinion will continue to support the Government if there are casualties in any numbers.

Many MPs feel that both sides are now engaged in a war of nerves.

Even if neither side seeks to provoke a conflict, accidental clashes could escalate the crisis.

The War Cabinet was examining the latest Argentine pronouncements to see if the door has been shut on further negotiations.

Some MPs feel the best hope lies with the United Nations, possibly by a direct intervention by the Secretary General, who is a Peruvian.

But Argentina's claim to sovereignty over the Falklands and Downing Street's commitment to self-determination for the islanders were still being seen as the crucial obstacle.

Bishop calls for peaceful solution

THE Bishop of Manchester today called for a peaceful settlement in the South Atlantic as the Falklands crisis appeared to be close to a violent climax.

"I don't believe an armed invasion would achieve our two objectives of upholding the rule of law and safeguarding the lives, freedom and property of the islanders," he said.

"There could be untold dangers in such an invasion when the devastating power of modern weapons and the facts of distance are taken into account.

"Every possible pressure should be brought on the British Government to continue to use means other than military to ensure that Argentine aggression is ended and a satisfactory long-term solution worked out.

DIVIDED

"If this would involve loss of face for our Government and country it would be better than the loss of many lives in the grim conditions of the South Atlantic.

"Efforts to secure the support of the United Nations have not yet been pursued to the limit. A UN peace-keeping force on the islands would be a better temporary solution than the efforts to reimpose British sovereignty by force.

"Christians are always divided over the use of armed force but those who are not pacifists can only back such methods when the foreseeable results would not offend justice and humanity more than the situation in which we find ourselves now. This cannot be so in the Falklands."

Test tube twins are doing fine

BRITAIN'S first test tube twins, Daniel and Christopher Smith, were pronounced "healthy" today as they lay in their incubators.

They were born six weeks ahead of their scheduled NHS delivery at London's Royal Free Hospital.

Proud mother Josephine, aged 31, from Aldersgate Road, Hike End, Stockport, was all smiles as she rested in a single-bed room. She had been in labour for 17 hours.

"I think that she has already breast-fed her babies," said a delighted hospital secretary, Mr Harry Oubridge.

The twins, born within 10 minutes, just before midnight, are the first test tube babies delivered on the NHS, he said.

Daniel weighed 4lb 10oz and Christopher 5lb 3oz.

The twins are being monitored in the hospital's special baby care unit. "They are not in danger, nor are they wired up," said Mr Oubridge.

"They are both in a healthy state," he added. "The mother is very well and very happy."

Josephine arrived at the hospital more than a fortnight ago.

"We wanted to have her in a couple of months in advance of the births," explained Mr Oubridge.

"It is not unusual for twins to be born prematurely."

There had been no special problems during the deliveries supervised by Prof Ian Craft without any call for a Caesarian section.

The twins' father, Mr Stuart Smith, a postman, was in the middle of his daily round when the news was broken to him that his own very special delivery was on the way.

His boss, sub postmaster Mr Derek Rawlinson, said Stuart's immediate reaction was: "Oh my God, it's happening."

Mr Rawlinson said: "The twins weren't due until early in June. Yesterday Stuart was out on a van run when the phone went.

"I took the call from a lady in the hospital's medical team. She sounded absolutely desperate and said that Stuart must be told as soon as possible that his wife was going into labour. I left a message for Stuart because I thought I may have to go out of the office, but he returned while I was still there. He was going frantic. He had no money with him, so we gave him some cash to get him on his way and he was off like a shot.

"All he could say was 'Oh my God'."

Stuart has worked from the Poynton office for about three years since he transferred from Stockport.

Mr Rawlinson added: "He's a tremendous lad. This couldn't have happened to a nicer couple. We are all tremendously delighted for Stuart and Jo, and I am sure that all the people on his round will be equally happy for him."

Stuart's mother, who lives in Dombey Close, Poynton, declined to say anything.

The test-tube birth technique involves fertilising the female egg outside the mother and then implanting it in her womb.

Britain mastered the art first when Mr Patrick Steptoe and Dr Robert Edwards helped produce the world's first test tube baby, Louise Brown, who was born at Oldham in the summer of 1978.

And talking of twins ...

Perishers locked in a tight spot

EVERYONE but the Army was called in to help when the terrible Bowmer twins struck again—and imprisoned themselves for nearly two hours.

By DAVID THOMAS

The panic started after haulage firm boss Stuart Bowmer left the 23-month-old twins in his £15,000 American sports car while talking to a friend at the roadside.

Youngsters Stuart and James leapt into the front seat and CLUNK pressed the automatic door locking button — with the only set of keys still in the ignition.

BRRMM, BRRMM, they went, pretending to drive the 150 mph Corvette Stingray as dad puzzled how to get them out. Soon the horn was sounding and radio blaring as they fiddled with every switch in sight.

A large crowd gathered in New Street, Milnrow, near Rochdale, offering ideas. All the windows were firmly shut. It was impossible to smash them for fear of hurting the children and the windscreen could not be removed because it is sealed.

More people gathered round, the police were called and then the fire brigade. Friends and relatives tried to coax the children to unlock the doors without success.

Meanwhile, they were happily tucking into a tube of indigestion tablets, which meant drastic action was necessary. But freedom came just as firemen were about to chisel through the car roof.

Mr Bowmer borrowed a screwdriver to force a narrow gap above the door window. James pulled the keys from the ignition and passed them through.

Mr Bowmer said: "A duplicate key would have been the answer, but they are impossible to obtain. I have tried before."

At home in Newhey Road, Newhey, near Rochdale, Mrs Jennifer Bowmer, aged 31, told of the twins' previous escapades. James pushed a chair through a glass door and smashed a window with his head.

Baby Stuart had a paddle after emptying chip pan oil over the kitchen floor, he put toy cars in the washer and stuffed sweet papers in the cassette player.

And both just love cleaning the windows with jam butties.

Mrs Bowmer said: "We never know what they'll do next — they are terrors. But they are just typical boys — and we love them."

Villa fined—but final spot safe

By PAUL HINCE

ASTON VILLA'S European Cup final place is safe . . . but the crowd riots which marred their semi-final against Anderlecht will cost the English champions £14,500 in UEFA fines.

Relieved Villa officials were informed early today that Anderlecht's protest had been rejected by a specially convened UEFA Commission which met in Zurich yesterday.

Anderlecht had claimed that an invasion of the pitch by Villa fans caused a direct interference with play and called on UEFA to either expel the English side from the European Cup or order the semi-final second leg to be replayed.

In imposing such a heavy fine, UEFA are clearly saying that Villa are responsible for their fans but did not think the incident serious enough to prevent the Midlands outfit facing Bayern Munich in the European Cup final on May 26.

However UEFA have also decided that Villa must play their next home European match behind closed doors. That game would take place next season providing Villa qualify for Europe by beating Bayern.

The UEFA Commission also decided that Anderlecht were partly to blame for the crowd disturbances and have fined the Belgian club £3,000.

Clive to the rescue

Fireman Clive Moss rescued a drowning pub from the River Douglas at Wallgate, Wigan.

He said "By its condition it looked like it had spent the night there. But after we fed it and gave it some milk, it began to look better." The pub is awaiting collection at Wigan police station.

Raiders beaten off

Four masked raiders were beaten off by postmen when they attacked a sorting office in Manchester today.

The masked men, armed with coshes and pickaxe handles struck as a security van was being loaded up at the New Street sorting office in Miles Platting.

Only one of the postmen was slightly injured and the attackers fled when the bandit alarm was activated. Nothing was stolen.

STOP PRESS

2

Clore's £28m

Tycoon Sir Charles Clore, who died in July 1979, left £28,300,000 gross (£14,879,000 net).

Royal opening

Princess Anne opened a £70,000 riding centre for the disabled at Cheltenham race course.

MANAGER SACKED

Bristol City today sacked manager Roy Hodgson who has been in charge at Ashton Gate for only four months.

SALE CYCLES WAREHOUSE

HALF PRICE BIKE SALE

FINAL WEEK
STOCK LIQUIDATION
SUPER QUALITY FULL SIZE
SPORTS METALLIC BLUE

List £140 — Half Price only £70

NEW RALEIGH BMX NOW IN STOCK

PLUS ALL RALEIGH & CARLTON MODELS AT HUGE SAVING

SALE CYCLES WAREHOUSE
435 Barlow Moor Rd, Chorlton, M/c 21
ACCESS, BARCLAYCARD & USUAL FACILITIES

NEW LOWER PRICE

Subject to availability

The Rain Shine Coat

Dashing trench to make sense out of summer showers. This one is grey, to make the day less so.

Budget showercoats from a selection of styles. Sizes 12-18 in shorter and average fittings. In light brown, green, blue and grey. Usually £22.99. **£19.99**

at Debenhams
MARKET STREET · MANCHESTER · Telephone: 832

They served in the Falklands

Wounded paratrooper, Ricky Westray, received a rapturous welcome when he returned home to Chadwick Road, Middlewich, Cheshire ahead of his unit from the Falklands.

Marines Paul Griffin (left) and Russell Smith were in the first wave of troops to storm ashore in the battle of the Falkland Islands.

Paratrooper Paul Dale was pictured handing back the Union Flag to residents of Broughton House, the East Lancashire home for disabled soldiers and sailors, in Salford. Paul's family had borrowed the flag to add a patriotic touch to his welcome home street party.

More street parties… and relatives, neighbours and friends greet John Davies, HMS *Coventry* survivor, as he arrives home.

Mark Anderson, a chef on the carrier HMS *Hermes*, was feted at a party in his honour when he returned from the Falklands.

Our Hero... Royal Marine Stephen Stoddard, serving with 42 Commando, got a rousing welcome home from friends and relatives of Radnor Avenue, Denton, when he returned from the Falklands.

Neighbours turned out to greet returning Falklands Commando Chris Oakes, aged 19, of Shepherd Cross Street, Bolton, with a street party. Chris, based at Seaton in Plymouth, returned home on *Canberra*.

A FRIEND DROPPING IN

LATE CITY

Manchester Evening News

36,140   BRITAIN'S BIGGEST REGIONAL NEWSPAPER   THURSDAY, AUGUST 22, 1985   17p

Ringway jet fireball: 54 die

PATHWAY TO DOOM — *black smoke billows from the stricken jet in this dramatic picture taken by a Manchester Evening News reader from the tarmac at Ringway.*

FIFTY - FOUR people were killed in a minute of horror today when a holiday jet burst into flames at Manchester Airport.

There were 83 survivors.

An explosion in the four-year-old Boeing's 737's port engine severed the aircraft's fuel lines and saturated it in fuel. Within seconds the aircraft had burst into flames.

Two stewardesses were thought to be among the dead.

The Civil Aviation Authority said this afternoon that it could not rule out the possibility of its demanding safety checks of all Boeing 737s held by airlines in this country.

The British Airtours Boeing bound for Corfu with 137 people aboard caught fire as it was about to take off.

There were 129 passengers and two babies with six crew members.

A police spokesman said: "The whole tragedy took place within a minute."

The pilot had radioed air traffic control saying he was having difficulty with the engine.

The majority of the dead were sitting in the rear section of the aircraft. The heat from the fire on the wing was so powerful it burned through the fuselage.

More disaster news and pictures.
Pages 2, 3, 4, 5, 30 and 31.

TRAGIC END *of holiday flight KT 328. Firemen battle to put out the flames*

TRY **LEYDEN** 1 ST for NISSAN

BROS LTD (CITY CENTRE) est 1947

HOLIDAY WEEKEND SPECIAL OFFER.
SCOOP PURCHASE OF CHERRY L ECLIPSES CUSTOMISED WITH SUN ROOF. ON THE ROAD AT EX WORKS COST OF

ONLY   **£4795**   ALSO   FABULOUS   DEALS   ON BLUEBIRDS AND SILVIAS

Massive Used Car Sale

£500 Discount if no Part Ex on quality used cars. Terrific selection. Open all holiday weekend.

B reg SUNNY 1.3GS 4-dr, 11,000 miles   £4495
W reg MINI, Yellow, lady owner 32,000 miles   £1895

LEYDEN BROS LTD
BLACKFRIARS CORNER, SALFORD 3
Sales & Service 061-832 3636
Spares 061-832 3062

NISSAN DEALER NISSAN   DEALER NISSAN DEALER

INSIDE   *Weather 2; Diary 6; Postbag 8; Lucky Addresses 12; BMDs 16; Business 17-18; Cartoons 34; Sport 56-60*   **TV** *32-33.*

The headlines say it all – and the dramatic picture taken by a reader speaks volumes.

Poignant moments – Prime Minister Margaret Thatcher visits the scene of the crash.

From the left – Debbie Wilson, Harry Wardle, Claire Bailey, Mike Mather, Marke Tatlock and Alison Hughes are six of the survivors of the Manchester air disaster of September 1985. Many people died after inhaling smoke when fire broke out on the Boeing 737. The six youngsters who had been out collecting money for the disaster fund handed over a cheque for £148 to John Bentley of the National Westminster Bank.

Seventy firemen tackled a blazing mill in Lower Broughton. It took four hours to bring it under control in March 1982.

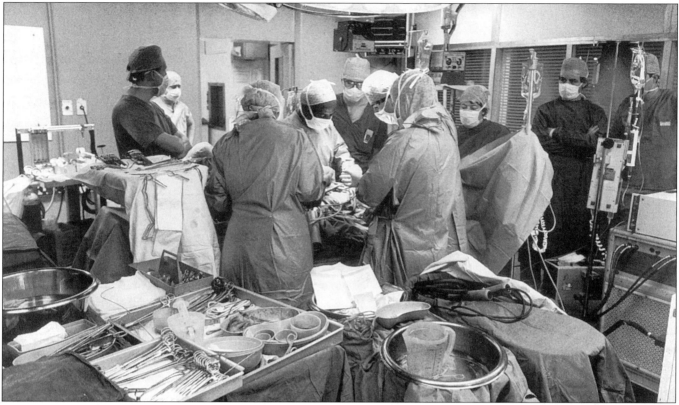

Evening News photographer John Fox and reporter Peter Harris were allowed to scrub up, don gowns and watch the first heart transplant at Wythenshawe Hospital. At 4:15am on April 11, 1987, a team of 20 led by Mr Ali Rahman, Consultant Cardio-Thorasic Surgeon at Wythenshawe Hospital, gently placed the new heart into the patient.

In 1982, Queen Elizabeth and the Duke of Edinburgh pay a visit to *Coronation Street* and meet the stars of this Granada Television drama.

We had some great children's parties at the Circus when it came to Belle Vue. The children here meet the clowns before the performance.

A 'Variety Show for the Elderly' was held each year at the Free Trade Hall and organised by Dave Eager and his friends from the entertainment world. Visiting celebrities such as Eartha Kitt, Emile Ford, Karl Denver and Stuart Hall have entertained our delighted senior citizens.

Capital of entertainment

Manchester has a great tradition in music – from the Hallé Orchestra to pop groups such as Simply Red, Take That or Oasis. Live musical entertainment for everyone! There are also musical schools such as Chethams. Chetham's hospital school was founded by Humphry Chetham, a Manchester Grammar School boy, who became a manufacturer of woollen cloth and a moneylender, amassing a great fortune. He became very prominent and in 1648 opened negotiations to establish a school in Manchester for the education and maintenance of forty 'poor boys'. It is now one of the greatest specialist music schools in the world. The original building is still intact, but additional buildings have been added to house the growing number of pupils. The students below celebrate Founders Day in 1957 and dress appropriately for a service at Manchester Cathedral.

The Duchess of Kent stops to look at some instruments in the glass cases in the library of the Northern College of Music, Manchester, in June 1973, after the official opening. She is currently President of the college which is now the Royal Northern College of Music.

The Hallé Orchestra in concert at The Free Trade Hall. The Orchestra was formed by Sir Charles Hallé who also created the Royal Manchester College of Music. The orchestra, Britain's oldest professional orchestra, was formed in 1858.

Manchester-based BBC Philharmonic is now one of Europe's finest orchestras. Guest conductor John Hopkins, on the right, rehearses the orchestra in 1989. He was formerly the principal conductor with the orchestra in the fifties. With him is Trevor Green, Head of Music, BBC North.

1983 and the Hallé's brass and percussion section play the *Fanfare for the Common Man* on the steps of the Town Hall, Manchester, to announce their 125th birthday appeal.

Popular music of the sixties and Manchester played its part; the first *Top of the Pops* was broadcast on New Year's Day, 1964, from a converted church in Dickenson Road, Rusholme. Around this time, Harpurhey lad Freddie Garrity formed Freddie and the Dreamers, seen here at rehearsal.

Another local group, Herman's Hermits was formed in 1963.

1966 – Eric Haydock, guitarist with the Manchester-based group The Hollies, pictured with his wife.

A 1993 picture of Derek Leckenby, of Herman's Hermits, with student Phil Holden before Derek and Barry Whitman joined North Area College, Heaton Moor, Stockport in a fund-raising concert.

The nineties and Steven Morrissey, Mancunian wordsmith and former frontman of the successful eighties band The Smiths, appears at the Apollo, Manchester.

Another Manchester group, Happy Mondays, at a Cities in the Park concert in 1991.

At the *News* Search for a Star contest in 1981 the winner was a young lady from Rochdale – 14-year-old Lisa Stansfield. *And right:* Now a superstar, Lisa Stansfield wows the audience in a concert a G-Mex.

Manchester heart-throbs Take That on stage at the Nynex Arena without group member Robbie Williams who had already left to pursue a solo career. The group eveunatally disbanded at the height of their fame in 1996 to the distress of their many young fans.

Mick Hucknall of Manchester group Simply Red entertains a Euro '96 crowd at Old Trafford.

Liam and Noel Gallagher of super group Oasis performing at G-Mex.

Students from South Manchester College with their window display at Manchester Museum for the Festival of Expressionism in 1992.

Dr Rosalie David, keeper of Egyptology at Manchester Museum, pictured in 1989. The museum has one of the leading collections of Egyptology and Dr David has headed the research team since 1972.

March 1983 and two-year-old Benjamin Green is dwarfed by the Avro Shackleton aircraft which dominates the aircraft museum in Liverpool Road, Manchester. Benjamin was getting a sneak preview of the museum before the official opening. The Air and Space Museum is part of the Castlefield Urban Heritage Park.

Moving into the Museum of Science and Industry is one of the nasties from TV's *Dr Who*, a Cyberman.

Two jugglers on unicycles perform during Castlefield Carnival, part of the Arts and Television Festival, which attracts thousands of visitors to the city in September.

A party of children arriving for an enjoyable day at this Lower Byrom Street warehouse, which forms part of the Manchester Museum of Science and Industry.

Lowry and his matchstick men

A well-known figure in Manchester until his death in February 1976, Laurence Stephen Lowry, was a gentle, unassuming man who was surprised by his fame. Born in Manchester in 1887, this painter concentrated largely on transferring to canvas his impressions of the city and its surroundings. His 'matchstick figures' set against backgrounds of factories and football grounds are unmistakable although many have tried to copy this style. *Photograph by Maurice Hatton of Camera Press, London.*

Greater Manchester is rich in public and private art galleries. Visitors are attracted to them not only for the wonderful paintings, but for events such as this auction at Manchester City Art Gallery in 1991.

Glitter of theatreland

The theatre in Greater Manchester is second to none, Bolton, Oldham, Tameside all have thriving theatres and Manchester can boast of the Palace Theatre (above) and the Opera House for the big scale ballet and operatic productions, plus such superb musicals as *Les Miserables* and *42nd Street*, the chorus for which lines up on stage on the right. The city also has the Contact and Library theatres, The Green Room and Nia Centre.

Warren Clarke (left) who plays Bosco and Paul Chapman as Harwell Mincing get ready for the shooting of Granada's Christmas show in 1986, *The Antelope Christmas*. Warren was a messenger boy at the *Manchester Evening News* who was always mimicking people and finally decided to go into acting.

A celebrity knees-up by stars who have appeared at the BBC Playhouse theatre in Hulme where many took their first steps to stardom. From left to right, Harry Worth, Cardew Robinson, Bill Waddington, The Beverley Sisters and Tom Mennard.

Cameron Mackintosh brought his hit musical *Les Miserables* to the Palace Theatre, Manchester, in April 1992 where it played to capacity audiences. The cast pose for a photo-call on stage.

The *Manchester Evening News Theatre Awards* started in 1982, to recognise the importance of theatre in Greater Manchester. A few famous faces from award ceremonies during the twelve years are featured here. On the right is Nicholas Parsons, who has compered the ceremony so brilliantly and professionally since 1988. With him is veteran actress Joan Turner. Below right is *Coronation Street's* Sarah Lancashire (Raquel) with Linus Roache. Below on the left is actress Susannah York together with the late Paul Eddington of *Yes Prime Minister* fame and immediately above is Tracy Dawson and daughter Charlotte. They accepted the Horniman Award made posthumously to comedian Les Dawson. As a final accolade to the importance of theatre in the region, Manchester was chosen as City of Drama 1994.

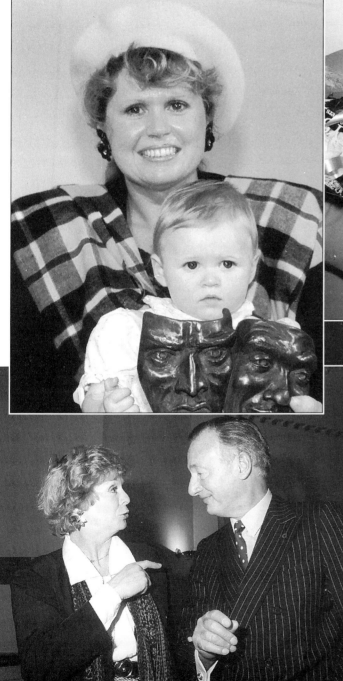

Those were the days – when City won the Cup in 1934.

NEVILLE BOLTON – Sports Editor of the *Manchester Evening News*.

Sport is the heartbeat of the North-West region and the *Manchester Evening News* has always been the taker of that mighty pulse.

Old Trafford football and cricket grounds and Maine Road have all been the stages for some of the greatest events in sport and homes to a host of undying legends.

There was the tragedy of the Munich Air Disaster in which eight of the famous Manchester United Busby Babes lost their lives; the glory of United's 1968 European Cup triumph and the FA Carling Premiership Trophy triumphs in 1993, 1994 and 1996. Manchester City have had their magic moments, too, they won the League Championship title in 1968, the FA Cup in 1969 and the League Cup and European Cup-winners' Cup in 1970.

The area is packed with the best in almost every other major sport. St Helen's and Wigan lead the way in Rugby League, top tennis stars play at Didsbury, world championship boxing is regularly staged at Manchester's Nynex Arena and G-Mex, and the superstars of golf are regular visitors to a region which has one of the greatest concentration of courses in the world.

Whatever the major – or minor – event and wherever big news is happening, the *Manchester Evening News* and *Pink* sports teams, two of the most experienced and respected in the business, have always been right in the thick of the action.

The northern Rugby League clubs are hard to beat. Pictured here are Swinton, who have just won the 1963 League Championship.

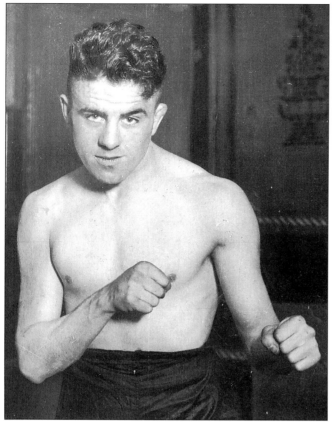

Jackie Brown from Manchester was the British and Empire, European and World Flyweight Champion in 1932.

Johnny King, with his Lonsdale Belt, fought for the Bantamweight world title in 1933.

King George V makes the first Royal visit to the provinces for a football match. The occasion was Manchester City v Liverpool on March 27, 1920 at City's ground, which was then in Bennett Street, off Hyde Road.

Jock McAvoy, British Middle and Lightweight Champion, who fought for the world title in 1936.

Peter Kane was World Flyweight Champion in 1938. Here he poses with Gracie Fields who presents him with his title belt.

Salford win the Rugby League Challenge Cup in 1938-39. Albert Gear, Salford, scores the winning try against Barrow at Wembley.

Najib Daho, who fought for the Super Featherweight world title in 1986, was tragically killed in a car crash in 1993.

Pat Barrett who fought for the world light welterweight title in 1991.

No, not Haydock Park Racecourse, where Lester Piggott rode his first winner in 1948, or Aintree, home of the Grand National. This was Manchester's own racecourse, Castle Irwell. The last race was run in 1963.

United become the first English team to win the European Cup in May 1968. Bobby Charlton – one of the original 'Busby Babes', survivor of the Munich crash and already a soccer legend – and Shay Brennan with the Cup aloft lead their victorious team round the Wembley ground.

Before the European Cup match in 1968 a solemn Bobby Charlton leads his team on to the pitch. Behind Charlton are Alex Stepney, Brian Kidd, George Best with the ball at his feet, John Aston, Billy Foulkes (half hidden), Tony Dunn and David Sadler.

British football's most controversial figure in 1971 and every boy's hero, George Best at a training session.

The 'Blues' let the world know about it! They have won the European Cup Winners Final at Vienna winning 2-1 against Gornik Zabrze. From the steps of the Town Hall, Manchester, in front of cheering fans, the ebullient Francis Lee takes over as cheer leader, joined by Malcolm Allison, holding the Cup and Mike Summerbee on the right with Tony Book behind. 'Franny' Lee returned to the club in the nineties – and purchased it!

Flashback to 1956 where we see the Manchester City 'Blues' returning to a civic reception at the Town Hall, Manchester after beating Birmingham 3-1 to win the FA Cup.

Weightlifting champion David Mercer of Tyldesley winner of a gold medal at the 1987 European Championships.

Reg Harris, of Bury, dominated sprint cycling in the post war years winning five world titles between 1947 and 1954. He also won two silver medals at the 1948 Olympics in London.

Brian Duncan, a local bowling champion from Bamber Bridge, who has won the Waterloo Handicap five times.

Manchester City pre-season photocall, August 1973. The club hit the headlines in 1993 when the management was challenged and criticism came from supporters and previous players, including millionaire Francis Lee (bottom left).

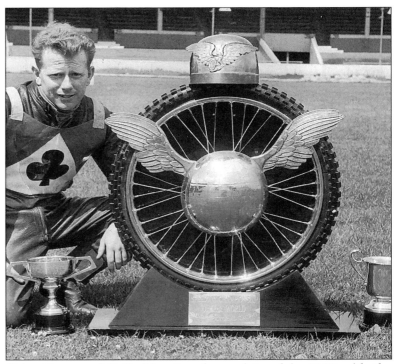

Radcliffe's John Spencer won the world professional snooker championship in 1969, 1971 and 1977.

Peter Craven of Belle Vue Speedway pictured in 1963 with the World Individual Championship Trophy, the Golden Helmet Match Race Trophy and the Match Race Championship Trophy. He also won the championship in 1955.

Picture of an annual top football club photocall: Manchester United lining up in 1975.

Peter Collins is welcomed home by both family and friends after winning the World Individual Speedway Championship in 1976.

Far left: Martin Grimley, one of the 1987 England World Cup hockey squad.

Left: Neil Fairbrother, the Lancashire and England cricketer pictured in 1987.

Below: Manchester 100 metre hurdler Shirley Strong, aged 24, preparing in 1984 for the Los Angeles Olympics where she won a silver medal.

Right: Ernest Tyldesley was a Lancashire County cricketer in the golden years of the twenties. His brothers Dick and James also played for the county.

Far right: Andrew Murray, who won the European Open Golf Championship in 1989.

Close friends Diane Edwards and her Sale Harriers' team-mate Ann Williams came first and second in the 800 metres final in the Commonwealth Games in Auckland in 1990 winning the gold and silver medals. At their joyful return to England they are greeted at Manchester Airport by 18-month old Nadine, niece of Di Edwards. Pictured from left to right are Paula Dunn another silver medal winner, Di Edwards (now Diane Modal), Nadine and Ann Williams.

Far left: Eric Evans is having a bit of fun with Manchester United centre-forward Tommy Taylor at Old Trafford football ground in 1958. Evans captained England at Rugby Union 1948 to 1958.

Left: Fran Cotton of Sale also captained The Lions during the years he played for England (1972 to 1981) – and provides the current team with their shirts!

Dewi Morris, Orrell and England scrum-half and his wife Penny are congratulated on their wedding by England and British Lions team-mates in August 1993.

Right: Another British Lions' captain, Tony Neary was at one time the most capped England player. He left the International scene with 46 caps.

Far right: Billy Beaumont, as captain of the England Rugby Union team, runs on to the field to the delight of the crowd in 1981. He is now more widely known for TV's *A Question Of Sport.*

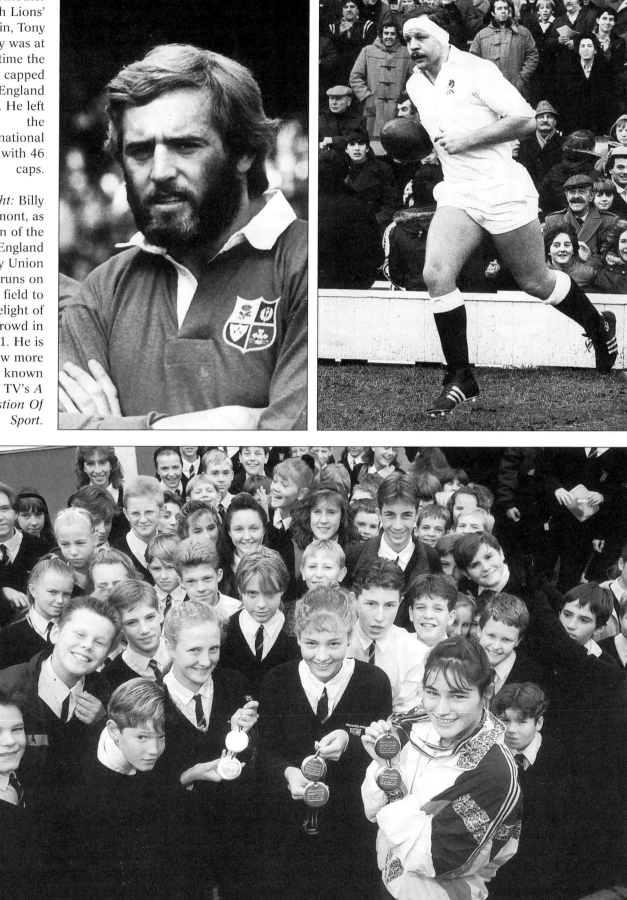

14-year-old Sarah Bailey from Disley competed successfully in the Barcelona Paralympics in 1991 winning two gold, three silver and two bronze medals. She was also the *MEN* Sports Personality of the Year in 1992. She is showing off her medals to schoolfriends at Poynton High School.

Wigan parade the Rugby League Championship trophy for their fans in 1987.

And in January 1996, they win the Regal Trophy Final at Huddersfield, captained by Shaun Edwards (back row, centre) – the most decorated Rugby League player in history. (Picture by Andrew Yates). With eight successive Challenge Cup trophies and seven Championship Cups to their credit, Wigan must be are the greatest Rugby League team of all time.

Captain of St Helens, Bobbie Goulding holds the first Stones European Super League Trophy aloft. In 1996 the team toppled Wigan RLC by winning this trophy, and the Silk Cut Challenge Cup.

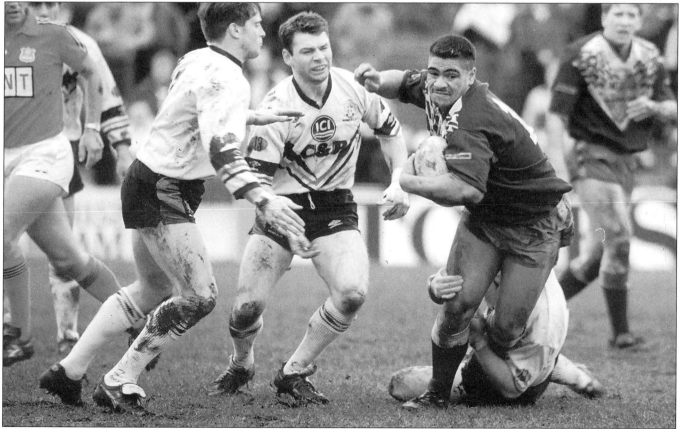

Rugby League and Swinton v Widnes in 1992. Swinton's Joe Faimolo is halted by Widnes' Alan Tait and David Hulme

Cricket and Dominic Cork of Derbyshire celebrates the first test hat-trick for England since Peter Loader 1957 in the England v West Indies final test at Old Trafford in 1995.   *Picture Andrew Yates*

Captain Mike Atherton hits out for 50 in a Lancashire v Durham Sunday game in 1993. Mike has captained England from 1994. His steady leadership and batting consistency could see him break Peter May's record for captaining England when he returns from the 1997 winter tour.

Lancashire beat Northamptonshire in the 1996 Benson and Hedges Cup Final and skipper Mike Watkinson holds aloft the trophy. Lancashire also added to their collection, thrashing Essex in the NatWest Trophy Final at the end of the season.
Picture Corey Ross/Action Images

Boxers Ensley Bingham (left) with his British Light Heavyweight Championship belt and Steve Foster with his IBF belt at the 1995 *MEN* Sports Awards.

At the same 1995 MEN Sports Awards , Sandy Busby, son of the late Sir Matt Busby who died in 1994, presents the Sir Matt Busby Award for Outstanding Services to Sport to Sir Bobby Charlton

In July 1995, Manchester's stunning, new £56m sports and entertainment complex, built next to Victoria Station , was opened to the public. Seating up to 19,500 people, the Nynex Arena has hosted a galaxy of stars including Pavarotti, Take That, magician David Copperfield, the World Table Tennis Championships and has regular sports events. In the same year, Manchester Giants made the Arena their home following a successful season at Manchester Velodrome. In this picture by Andrew Yates, 6ft 5in Mark Robinson outstretches his opponents to the basket.

Like beings from outer space, the full drama of ice hockey comes to Manchester as the players enter the Arena accompanied by the special effects of dry ice, music and light. Manchester Storm's net minder Colin Downie is framed in the entrance tunnel.

Manchester
Storm in
action on the
ice.
*All Ice Hockey
pictures by
Andrew Yates.*

… and posing
victorious for
the camera.

Another trophy for Manchester United! Manager Alex Ferguson (left), captain Eric Cantona and assistant manager Brian Kidd hold the FA Cup after victory at Wembley. This clinched the double in 1996.

Former Manchester City managers, John Bond (left) and Brian Horton welcome the Euro '96 Championships to Manchester.

Olympic and Paralympic athletes are honoured at Stockport Town Hall. On the back row from left to right – swimmer James Hickman, Paralympic swimmer Sarah Bailey, who won three gold, two silver and one bronze medal in Atlanta to add to her growing collection, Olympic swimmer and silver medalist Graeme Smith and Paralympic Team Manager, Tony Sainsbury. On the front row from left to right are Rachel Potter, Paralympic Pentathlon and Bill Curran, Paralympic Bowls.

In August 1996 the World Track Cycling Championships were held at the purpose built Manchester Velodrome and here we see Chris Boardman from Hoylake as he shatters the world record for the 4,000 metres pusuit with a time of 13 minutes, 353 seconds.

Gathering the news

PAUL HORROCKS – Deputy Editor and former News Editor of the *Manchester Evening News* gives us an insight into the news gathering operation of a newspaper.

HARD NEWS... It's the lifeblood of newspapers, and one of the main reasons why most people buy the *MEN*.

We carry local, national, and international news, gathered by our own team of reporters and photographers, backed by correspondents all over the world. It's a fast and aggressive business, but never dull.

We reflect people's lives, their dreams and their tragedies.

Time is the enemy. With five editions per day, each requiring updated information as stories change or new ones break, deadlines have to be met. The paper won't wait.

News reporters rush out of court to file a story with minutes to spare before the next edition is completed. Often there's no time to even sketch an outline of the story – it's straight on to the telephone and dictate copy from shorthand notes.

Complicated facts have to be marshalled into an easy to follow style.

Photographers must calculate just how much time to wait at the scene of a crime or at a football match, before leaving for the office to process their pictures. Fast moving technology means that sometimes pictures can be transmitted by phone line, and reports filed on lap top computers.

But where do all the different stories come from? The *MEN* newsroom puts in dozens of calls each day to the emergency services. Contacts built up over years are checked by our specialist writers. And the greatest source of information – our own readers – call the newsdesk to tell us something new. No two days are ever the same.

I spent 15 years as an on the road reporter, and saw things and met people I shall never forget.

When the Moors murder inquiry reopened at Saddleworth I was the paper's crime correspon-

Paul Horrocks (centre) at an interview given by search chief Peter Topping in 1987.

dent and spent hours in the pouring rain waiting for details of the police operation. Finally, when Myra Hindley was brought back to the scene of her crime, hundreds of journalists were despatched to the desolate moor, in driving snow, to watch a distant figure in overalls and red gloves helping police in their grisly search for bodies.

The twisting and turning of the Stalker affair, its political intrigue and police secrecy was fascinating. But the pressure to be first with the latest development was wearing.

I shall never forget a Wednesday night in Lockerbie, just before midnight, walking along dark, winding, lanes littered with the shattered fragments of a Pan-Am jumbo jet, wondering how such a huge aircraft could be smashed into so many tiny pieces. The smell of aircraft fuel was heavy in the air.

In Zeebrugge harbour I joined a mob of journalists, all pushing to be first on board a tug to circle the overturned hulk of the *Herald of Free Enterprise* ferry in which 188 had died. Making notes from the quayside was one thing, but to get so close to a half-submerged ferry, lying on its side was an experience which silenced every one of us watchers.

As news editor I was indoors and the journalists file their reports to me to be checked and passed to the editor.

I am continually looking forward, trying to forecast which way a story will turn. It's like a game of chess, ensuring your team are in the right place at the right time to gain the maximum information in the most professional way. It's a hard game.

December, 1986 and after more than two decades, Myra Hindley returns to the scene of her horrific crime. She was helping police to trace the remaining graves on the desolate Saddleworth Moor.

A flashback to police on duty on the mist-covered moors near where the body of 10-year-old Lesley Downey was found in a shallow grave near the Greenfield to Holmfirth Road at Wessenden Head.

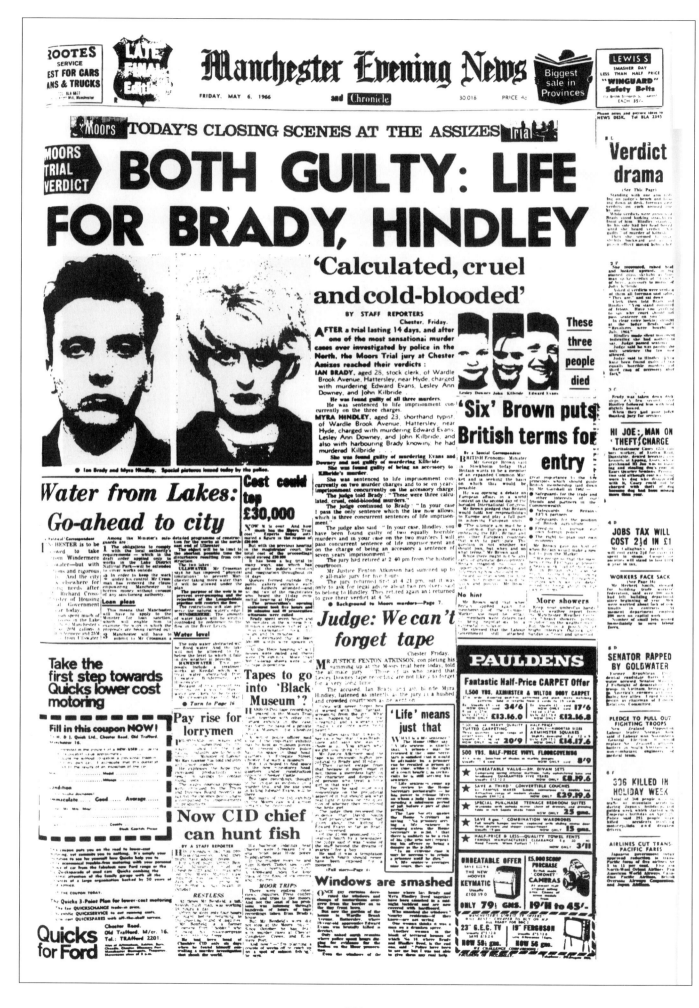

This shocking picture was taken by our photographer Eric Graham, unknown to the man who was threatening to strangle a woman hostage during a siege at a flat in Levenshulme. All press had been banned from the area. The woman was later released and the man arrested. The exclusive picture was used on the *MEN* front page and also in the national papers the following day. It was also useful to police as an aid to convicting the man of the crime.

Big cities all have their problems and unrest in Moss Side erupted in riot scenes in 1981. Shops were set alight and this dramatic picture was taken by Clive Cooksey.

Who would choose to be a policeman! Youths, one of them masked, menace police who are sheltering behind their riot shields. Some of the youths taunted the officers and, from the rear of this crowd, bricks were thrown. The reporting of such occasions in a fair, unbiased and accurate way is important. It is big news. People want – and need to know the facts. When a big news story breaks, the reporters and photographers get to the centre of the action.

At a press conference on June 25, 1986 John Stalker resigns as deputy chief constable of Greater Manchester.

The Stalker affair

There was much support in Manchester for John Stalker following his suspension from office in 1986. One of Britain's highest ranking policemen, he was taken off an inquiry into the Royal Ulster Constabulary. It was national news, but nowhere was it covered more fairly or accurately than in the *Manchester Evening News*.

Only a few months earlier, in March 1986, John Stalker, on the right, had been greeting the Queen at the Greater Manchester Police Headquarters. The Chief Constable of Greater Manchester, Jim Anderton, is on the left.

187

This is the city edition of the newspaper, which came out on the second day of Strangeways Prison riots. Britain's most serious prison disturbance broke out in the chapel on Sunday, April 1, 1990. By midday 1,000 prisoners were on the loose within the prison, fires were burning in several places and prison staff had withdrawn to secure the perimeter. Most inmates gave themselves up during the first 24 hours and only 120 remained inside by lunchtime on April 2. The events aroused immense public interest and received enormous coverage in the media. Horrific accounts of killings, butchery and torture appeared and, with the information that 20 'body bags' had gone into the prison, we feared the worst.

The Editor, Michael Unger, offers to act as mediator and is allowed into the prison to talk to the prisoners who confirmed that there were 'no dead'.

The remaining prisoners on the roof of the prison.

Prisoners on the roof of the prison, caught in the spotlight of the police helicopter, which continually circled the area. The siege lasted for 25 days. *Picture by* Guardian *photographer Denis Thorpe.*

In December 1992, IRA bombs went off in Manchester city centre. Office workers were evacuated from buildings and roads were cordoned off as police received confusing warnings from terrorists.

These people had just been evacuated from their shops and offices when a second bomb exploded. The shocked and injured are helped by passers-by.

This picture shows the mangled wreckage of the gas storage tanks in Warrington after an IRA attack in February 1993.

Police and troops set up road blocks near the site and hunt for clues to the bomb gang.

… And, if this was not enough, the town and whole nation were stunned by the attack on the Warrington shopping centre the following month. Johnathan Ball, three, and Tim Parry, twelve, were tragically killed by an IRA bomb and many people were badly injured. Hundreds of teddy bears and bunches of flowers were left at the scene to mark this shocking event.

MEN steps into the Nineties

NEW technology is very much in evidence in a modern newspaper office and the *Manchester Evening News* is no exception. The bright, air conditioned offices on Deansgate and the clean and spacious printing plant at Trafford Park are vastly different to the conditions even ten years ago. Here we see Editor Michael Unger (centre) and News Editor Paul Horrocks, now Deputy Editor, being interviewed by GMR presenter, Jeremy Dry (left) in 1992.

Equipped with the most up-to-date technology, a reporter keys in her story to the computer system.

A profile is discussed on the business desk for the daily business sction of the paper.

The next edition is planned and the news updated - there are five editions each day.

Colour photographs flow into our electronic picture desk from all over the world as well as from our staff and freelance photographers.

A reel of paper is collected from the paper store.

The pages are sent electronically to Trafford Park where the pages are received as negatives.

(*top left*) One of the micro-chip controlled robots delivers a reel of paper to the press. (*top right*) An aluminium plate is fitted to one of the Goss web-offset computer controlled presses. (*bottom left*) The presses roll and the completed papers are taken by conveyor belt to the publishing room, where they are automatically wrapped in bundles. (*bottom right*) The papers are collected by the drivers for distribution in the distinctive yellow and black vans.

The finished product is given a final check.

Into the Nineties

Visionary of the nineties Bob Scott (on the right) and Rick Parry of Ernst & Young, later to become Chief Executive of the Premier League, survey the land at Dumplington, which was to be the site of

one of the Olympic stadiums in March 1990. Bob first had the idea of bringing the Olympic Games to Manchester way back in 1984 and his sheer persistence and drive took us into bidding for the games for 1996 and the year 2000. After a truly magnificent bid for Britain, which has done so much for the North-West

and put Manchester firmly back on the map where it belongs, the IOC committee decided on September 23, 1993 that the Games for the year 2000 should go to Sydney, Australia. Mancunians were shocked and saddened at the result, but firmly believe that our team and their supporters in Monaco were true winners that day.

Princess Anne, supporter of the Manchester Olympic Bid and IOC member for Britain, with the managing director of Bovis, Dennis Bate, inspect the proposed arena site at Victoria Station.

A lone angler fishes in the canal as the structure of Manchester's Olympic Velodrome rises in the background.

Geoff Thompson, with five world karate titles under his belt, is now chairman of the North West Sports Aid Foundation, centred in Manchester, and was a roving ambassador for the Olympic Bid.

Announcing the British bid for the Year 2000 Olympics at a press conference, in February 1992 are, from left to right: the Duke of Westminster; Bob Scott who was the driving force behind the bid; Graham Stringer, Leader of the City Council; Robert Key, Minister for Manchester; Robert Atkins, Minister for Sport

The British Olympic bid team set off to fly to Lausanne to present their hi-tech bid to the Olympic Committee. Leading the way is 'Manchester', the Olympic Lion, with Bob Scott, Chairman of Manchester 2000, Bill Enevoldson Finance Director and Frances Toms Corporate Planning Manager.

Left: Airport staff celebrate the opening of Terminal 2 at Manchester International Airport with a bottle of champagne.

Above: Train-crazy Samuel Hilton, aged four, was the first to ride on Ringway's partially-completed Terminal 2 rail link.

March 1993 and the first holidaysmakers to use Terminal 2, crowd round to check in their luggage

Rail chiefs Michael Renshaw, Gordon Jakes and Richard Hill at the airport station of the rail link to the opening in 1993.

Concorde, the beautifully designed supersonic aircraft, rests at Manchester International Airport. *Photographed by Clive Cooksey, Deputy Picture Editor.*

A plane at the point of take-off at Manchester International Airport.

Trams return to Manchester. After 43 years rails are again laid in Manchester's streets for this hi-tech tramway system. Two Metrolink trams are seen passing each other at the junction of High Street and Market Street.

The Prime Minister John Major visiting British Aerospace at Warton near Preston early in 1993 covered his ears from the aircraft noise – or was it that he couldn't listen to more crticism. *Photographer – Mike Grimes.*

A kiss on the hand for Princess Diana during a visit to the city in 1991.

The Queen shares a smile with the people of Manchester on her walkabout when she visited the city in 1992.

Prince Charles poses for our cameraman, John Fowler at Ordsall Library where he was meeting Prince's Trust grant recipients and residents of Ordsall estate. Lynn May, our *MEN* journalist (in the check jacket), was a private guest of the Trust and afterwards wrote an exclusive feature about the visit and Prince Charles's work to help young people.

Manchester Evening News

FRIDAY, MAY 8, 1992   LATE CITY   30p

SHOCKING SHARON   WIN £43,000 ON SPOT THE BALL PAGE 50   **Queen of the fairways**

PAGE ONE COMMENT

Don't let Laura die

■ WAITING for a new life, little Laura Davies, four, smiles through her anguish. The operation she desperately needs is not available in Britain on the NHS and time is running out. Picture: JOHN FOWLER

Dear Mrs Bottomley,

Laura Davies is four years old. Her greatest wish is to be able to start school in September with her playmates.

But her wish may never come true. Laura is dying.

She was born with a rare bowel disorder, developed liver failure and has got only months to live.

You have the power to help save her life.

Generous

The double liver and bowel transplant operation she desperately needs is not yet available in Britain on the National Health Service but is being done successfully in America and doctors there are willing to operate on Laura.

But the surgery and after-care will cost a staggering £350,000. The generous

An open letter to new Health Secretary Virginia Bottomley

people of Greater Manchester have taken Laura, from Eccles, to their hearts and raised a magnificent £47,000 in just a few short weeks. Given time they would raise the rest.

But Laura Davies doesn't have that time.

Doctors say her small body is failing fast. The operation is her only hope. She cannot wait a decade for the same techniques to be developed here, cannot wait

for Britain to catch up, cannot wait for the NHS. She needs to go to America — and she needs to go NOW

Your health department says it is against the law for patients to be treated outside Britain on the NHS.

But rules can be changed. Alternatives can be found.

Your Government could and should give her the money. No-one in the country would begrudge this little girl a

penny. Mercifully most illnesses can be treated in Britain, but Laura is a rare case. Her parents know that if they had the money their daughter could be saved.

Imagine their anguish as time runs out. They are being denied the basic right of treatment for their daughter — because that treatment does not exist in this country.

Defied

For all her short life Laura has been fed through an intravenous drip. She has never had a birthday cake, never tasted ice-cream.

You cannot sit back and deny her the chance of a normal life, you cannot sit back and watch her die. Laura has defied the odds already — she has re-written the rules.

Now it is your turn.

Sue them, says US hospital: Page 3

IF there is ever any doubt about the generosity and warm-heartedness of people in the North-West, you only have to see the way they respond to an appeal for help, especially if that appeal is for a child. Little Laura Davies of Eccles captured all our hearts in 1992.

Born with a rare bowel disorder, at four years old she needed a double liver and bowel transplant to save her life. The *News* led the way – and our readers responded by collecting a massive £200,000 to send Laura to America for treatment. The story became national news and King Fahd of Saudi Arabia, in an amazingly generous gesture, gave the remaining £150,000 needed.

Laura eventually required further operations to replace vital organs and the moral issues were debated around the world. Tragically, she died in November 1993, aged five.

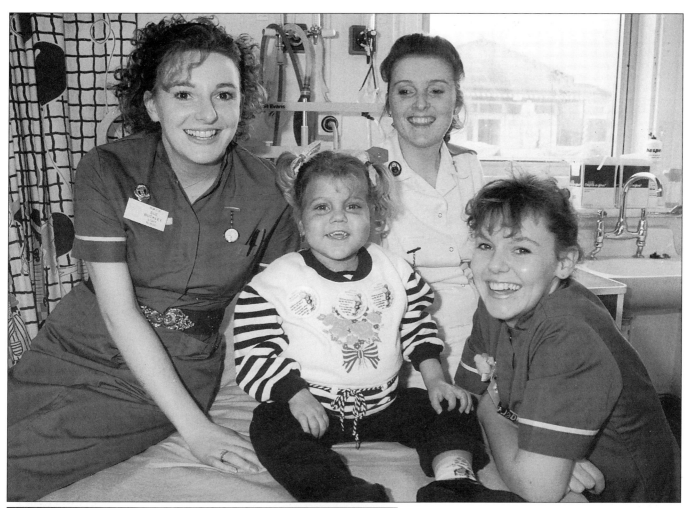

April 1992; Laura is pictured in Wakefield Ward of The Royal Manchester Childrens' Hospital, Pendlebury with her friends – from the left, Staff Nurse Sue Buckley, Staff Nurse Veronica McHugh and Staff Nurse Joanne Whitnall. *Photographer – Eric Graham.*

Charity begins at home

Another indefatigable fundraiser for Pendlebury Children's Hospital was Bryan Robson of Manchester United. The former MUFC captain set out to raise £1.5 million for a new scanner for the hospital. Here he tries his hand at making a pizza at the Domino Pizza shop in Swinton before taking a batch along for the patients at the hospital.

Saluting the heroes of 1945

IT WAS May 8, 1995 – 50 years after the end of World War Two in Europe. Thousands poured into Manchester to pay homage to the men and women who helped to make the original VE-Day possible.

Young and old joined a giant party celebration in Albert Square, the crowd in front of the town hall singing old favourites such as Vera Lynn's *We'll Meet Again.*

Other celebrations included special parades with bemedalled old comrades remembering the victims of the war. There were also scores of street parties in Manchester and Salford - just as there had been in 1945.

And amid the red, white and blue bunting and Union Jacks, a select band of Mancunians who had been born on May 8, 1945, raised their glasses to toast their 50th birthdays.

Other 50th anniversary celebrations in Manchester marked D-Day (the Normandy landings) and VJ-Day (the end of the war against Japan).

Back on parade, Burma Star Association members march to remember their fallen comrades.

These old soldiers, proudly wearing their medals, were among the thousands who remembered the horrors of World War Two.

Four views from the VJ-Day remembrance service at G-Mex. It was one of the most poignant of Manchester's anniversary celebrations.

Despite being confirmed to wheelchairs, these old soldiers were determined to take part in their 50th anniversary celebrations.

Ex-servicemen shed a tear for fallen comrades at the D-Day anniversary service in St. Peter's Square, Manchester.

Bunting baby: The people of Chadderton didn't have to guess where VE-Day baby May Victoria Barton lived - her house was covered in red, white and blue to mark her 50th birthday.

Dancing for joy, Beswick residents celebrate the anniversary of VE-Day at their party organised by the Doric Tenants and Residents Association.

Bloody — but unbowed

SATURDAY June 15, 1996.... a normal shopping day in Manchester with the city centre thronged with families, many buying cards and gifts for Father's Day. But at 11.15am an IRA bomb - 3,3000lbs of explosives in a Ford Cargo van - ripped the heart out of the city.

The blast was heard five miles away. Entire buildings, including a wall of the Arndale Centre, crumbled and windows were shattered half-a-mile away. More than 200 people were injured.

One of the miracles of that horrendouse day was that the police evacuated 80,000 souls without a single fatality.

It was the worst-ever peacetime bomb with insurers facing a £370m bill to get Manchester ticking again. But there was a gritty determination among the Manchester business community with council leader Graham Stringer declaring: "This cowardly attack by barbarians will not be allowed to damage the city in the way they want."

The bomb was a callous echo of the Mother's Day bombing in a Warrington shopping centre three years before when twelve-year-old Tim Parry and three-year old Jonathan Ball were killed.

By the end of 1996 the rebuilding of the bombed area was well under way.

The moment the bomb went off. Cross Street is eerily deserted, the shoppers having been cleared by police moments before.

Picture: News Team International

They bombed the heart out of Manchester's shopping centre, but true love was made of sterner stuff. Franklin Swanson and Amanda Hudson's wedding day was thrown into chaos. Amid the havoc of the day, the Moston couple's ceremony went ahead two hours late after the bride's hired Rolls-Royce was trapped outside the police cordon. Then they emerged from the register office – and into the confusion that gripped the city. Franklin, 30, and Amanda, 26, had to make a dash for it – and were pictured with bridesmaid Lucy Hudson. *Picture: Chris Gleave*

Warned by police, shoppers flee along Deansgate before the bomb exploded. *Picture: Carl Royle*

An aerial view of the devastation. Debris litters Corporation Street outside the wrecked frontage of Marks and Spencer.

The youngest victim: a woman follows in despair after handing her injured baby to an ambulanceman seconds after the blast.

Picture: Carl Royle

Hundreds of businesses were blitzed by the blast.

Splintered woodwork is all that is left of the front of this building

Workmen clear the debris just off Maket Street.

Manchester Evening News

Friday June 21 1996 · Founded 1868 · *A friend dropping in* · 30p · Final · SOCCER CITY 96

ROCK HARD CAGE — Now Nick's an action hero — CINEMA: Pages 50-51

Go MANCHESTER'S BEST ENTERTAINMENTS GUIDE — STARTS ON PAGE 35

RETURN OF THE HITMAN — Page 9

PAGE ONE COMMENT

Please help

Dear Prime Minister,

AT 11.15am last Saturday the IRA cowardly let off a huge bomb in our city centre where only minutes before 80,000 shoppers, workers and Euro 96 fans had been happily enjoying the summer sun.

The bombing caused outrage not only in Britain, but around the world. In the days since, Mancunians — helped by thousands of messages of support — have pulled together like never before to make sure that life returns to as near normal as possible as soon a possible.

Because as you can see in our picture the city centre looks like a Beirut war zone.

However only now is the true cost becoming known of the IRA's terrorism when the biggest ever bomb in mainland Britain wrecked Manchester's city centre.

● It will cost jobs: family firms will close, traditions will end. More than 150 small close-knit groups who had no terrorist insurance could go to the wall.

● It will cost at least £500m to repair the damage — and that figure could well rise.

● It will cost the enjoyment of city centre activities such as the Royal Exchange theatre, street performances and the simple pleasure of shopping.

You will receive reams of reports forecasting despondent business, massive insurance claims and chilling engineers' surveys that show the devastation in our city centre. But nothing can compare with a personal visit to see how badly we have been hit — because the very heart of the city now lies grievously wounded. Traders in the Arndale Centre have been deeply affected by the video of the internal damage to the complex. The film told them more, one said, than five days of meetings in Manchester Town Hall.

And it takes that personal insight to appreciate the destruction in the city centre. Thankfully, no-one died in the 3,300lb bomb that went off last Saturday. But this does not mean that we are not facing problems of a massive kind. And you can have no idea how bad things are until you see them.

Simply because no one died we fear that we will become another Westminster statistic and in a few weeks time forgotten by the Whitehall civil servants and London politicians who will, inevitably, get bogged down in bureaucratic red tape — arguing over small print: fighting over who pays for what: squabbling over whether or not Europe should help out. We need help, particularly, for the small family concerns, the one-off cafes and bars, the characters that pull us back time and time again into the Arndale, to the Royal Exchange and the Corn Exchange who have found themselves homeless and deserted.

■ LIKE a scene from Beirut . . . the devastation of Longridge House, Corporation Street, stripped of its facade

They valiantly turn up at the Town Hall every day to find out when they are likely to be given access to their shops and their stock — worrying about their future. We in this city have showed a remarkable team spirit over the past few days, but now is the time for the personal and moral support from the Prime Minister to reassure us that years of hard graft and investment are not wasted — lost in a puff of terrorists' smoke.

Home Secretary Michael Howard came on Monday to give succour to Manchester and to show defiance to the IRA, but it was not apparent at that time just how far-reaching the damage was — particularly to small firms who do not have the resources to allow their businesses to lie idle for weeks. This is not another bomb in the City of London, affecting multi-nationals and rich merchant banks. Could you perhaps consider setting up a special task force led by the Deputy Prime Minister to help out these firms?

There is no need for Ministers to fear they will set a precedent by providing special measures for compensation and job protection. And there is no need to fear that the publicity which will surround your visit will give the IRA even more succour. Because this evil attack on Manchester is out of our normal sphere of understanding and totally outrageous.

It needs the Prime Minister to come out of London and come to Manchester to prove that Britain will not cow to the threat of terrorism.

For the sake of the people of Manchester, please come.

Michael Unger,
Editor

Beef war ends in deal for Major

By Geoff Meade

THE British beef war is over, it was announced at the European Union summit in Florence today.

EU leaders unanimously approved a "framework" plan for the dismantling of the worldwide ban on UK beef exports on the basis of meeting health and scientific criteria.

John Major has accepted that the stage-by-stage removal of the ban will only be achieved after rigorous checks on public health standards by EU Commission experts.

But he can claim victory in wringing a last small concession from his partners before signing a deal he will now take home to sell to his Tory Euro sceptics.

The EU leaders also announced good news for Europe's — and Britain's — farmers in the form of an extra £160 million in cash support for beef producers.

The stages of today's agreement include:

● The lifting of the export ban on animals and meat from certified herds — those with no history of BSE, and no exposure to infected meat-and-bone meal.

● The lifting of the ban on cattle embryos.

Meat and Livestock Commission chairman Don Curry said tonight: "This is a vital step in putting British beef back on the menus of Europe." John Major had achieved "a breakthough."

Holiday alert

BRITONS going to France this weekend have been warned they face disruption after hundreds of tourists spent the night on a stranded ferry when French farmers, protesting over the mad cow crisis, refused to let it dock.

■ Full story: Page 6

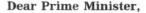
WEATHER 2 BMDs 64 DIARY 34 POSTBAG 44 TV 45-48 BUSINESS: 4 PAGES

The bomb hit the heart of the city and help was urgently needed. On June 21, the editor, Michael Unger, published an open letter to the Prime Minister requesting Government aid. The voice of the people was heard – as the headlines proclaimed on July 3. The Prime Minister had replied to the Editor and promised £21m cash help for Manchester.

Castlefield Carnival is now one of the city's most popular events and takes place in this wonderfully regenerated area of Manchester. Castefield's canals are again in use and the warehouses are converted into hotels, youth hostels and city dwellings.

One of the many canal boat owners – and his dog – enjoying the carnival.

A view of Castlefield showing rail, road and pedestrian bridges with boats moored in the foreground and city flats in the background.

Youngsters from Ordsall with a stilt-walker and uni-cyclist enjoy a new canalside walk in Salford. The walkway will eventually link Salford Quays with the heart of Manchester.

Mardi Gras revellers at 7am in G-MEX in August 1996.

A boat sails on calm water in front of the spectacular Salford Quays backdrop.

Another impressive view of Harbour City at Salford Quays for the annual University men's eights boat race, Manchester v Salford.

Kathryn Yates of the Sorrel String Quartet plays the violin in front of the new Bridgewater Hall in September 1996.

Prince Charles is shown the model of the proposed Commonwealth Games stadium site for Manchester in 2002.

The sound of the twenty-first century: the Hallé Orchestra gives their first public performance in their new home, the Bridgewater Hall.

Picture by Chris Gleave